VANISHING AMAZON

MIRELLA RICCIARDI

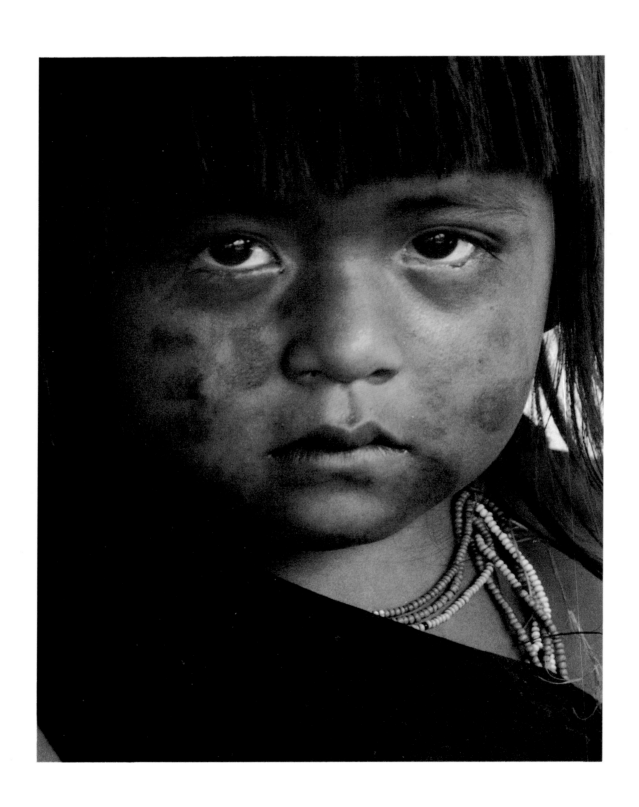

VANISHING AMAZON

MIRELLA RICCIARDI

with introductions by

Marcus Colchester

HARRY N. ABRAMS, INC., PUBLISHERS
NEW YORK

My journey to the Amazon and, in turn, the creation of this book would not have been possible without the understanding, kindness and practical help of my friends and colleagues. In particular I would like to acknowledge the generous support of **Peter Block** at **Kodak**; **Barry Taylor** at **Olympus** for the camera equipment which never let me down; **Guy Ashton** for his much-appreciated contribution of **Muesli Bars**; **Vamoose**, insect repellent; **Tony White** of **Black and White Photo Laboratories**; and **Honda Generators**. To all of these and many more unnamed I offer my heartfelt thanks.

Mirella Ricciardi's text and photographs © MIRELLA RICCIARDI 1991
Marcus Colchester's text and map © George Weidenfeld and Nicolson Ltd 1991

Library of Congress Cataloging-in-Publication Data
Ricciardi, Mirella.
    Vanishing Amazon / by Mirella Ricciardi.
        p.   cm.
    Includes index.
    ISBN 0–8109–3915–0
    1. Indians of South America—Amazon River Region—Social life and customs.   2. Indians of South America—Amazon River Region—Social conditions.   3. Man—Influence on nature—Amazon River Region.
    4. Amazon River Region—Social conditions   I. Title.
    F2519.1.A6R53   1991
    981′1—dc20   91–12108
                                                              CIP

Published in 1991 by Harry N. Abrams, Incorporated, New York
A Times Mirror Company

Map by LINE AND LINE
Designed by NICK AVERY
Edited by BARBARA MELLOR

Overleaf A Kampa child
Pages 8–9 Yanomami boys, their faces painted with traditional designs
Pages 12–13 A Yanomami hunter. Guns are slowly beginning to replace traditional bows and arrows and blowpipes

Photographs and engravings on pages 18–30, 40–1, 110–11 and 158–9 are reproduced by kind permission of the Royal Geographical Society.

Printed and bound in Italy

CONTENTS

"What you do to the earth you do to the sons of the earth."

American Indian saying

Departure

'So what was it like in the Amazon?' my friends all asked me when I returned from my three-and-a-half-month battle with Brazil. 'Awful,' was the word that first sprang to mind. They looked surprised. 'What do you mean, "Awful"?' I paused for a moment: how could I answer such a question in a word, or a sentence? Yes, it was awful – not wonderful, exciting, fantastic, enthralling, or any of those other adjectives that people tend to use when describing an unusual or exotic adventure. The Amazon, the rainforest, the South American Indians, the primeval trees: all these words conjured up mental images filled with a mystery that sets one dreaming. So why was it awful? I needed to pause and put my mind into reverse before continuing. 'Let me say that it was the toughest, most demanding ordeal I have yet faced.' It had not been at all what I had expected or imagined. The heat, the insects, the language barriers, the rough living conditions had all amply justified my worst apprehension and misgivings. But what I had not reckoned with were the very people I had set out to photograph, the Indians themselves.

The complexities entailed in the undertaking had defied my imagination, and perhaps because of that I had just held my breath amd jumped in at the deep end. How many times had I later asked myself, 'What am I doing here? Why do I get myself into such situations? What am I trying to prove?' After much reflection and soul-searching, I came to the conclusion that I was born with a hunter's instinct. Having been raised in Africa I am quite familiar with this trait. The trophy hunter was part and parcel of my youth, and now I came to recognize the same instinct in myself. Whether hunting for game trophies or for images, the impulse is the same. The prospect pushes you on in a mad obsessive search that knows no limits or constraints.

So, yes, ninety-five per cent of it was a tough, awful experience, full of agony and distress and frustration. But it was the remaining five per cent that kept me going, when I touched on or caught glimpses of the world I was trying to penetrate. This was what made me disregard the hardships and discomforts of the maddening, infuriating, interminable labryinth I had stepped into. I had moved into a world so far removed from mine that I could have been on another planet, and yet the people who lived there resembled me. It was what lay beneath the surface that so baffled me and that I had been unable to comprehend despite the many cautionary tales. Perhaps it's just as well. I might never have taken the plunge, and now that it is all behind me, of course I am glad I did.

So where do I begin? Perhaps by admitting that I am an incurable romantic, a victim of beauty in any form. My fantasies get the better of me and I am transported beyond reality and into the realms of illusion. When my bubble bursts I return to earth, impact brings me back to my senses and I realize that I was only dreaming.

I also know, however, that beauty lies in the eye of the beholder, and we are all free to choose the way we see. Somewhere deep inside me there lurked the knowledge that there may exist another world within the world we live in, where my fantasies could become a reality. So I set out to find it.

At an international meeting on the Amazon basin held in London I heard the words: 'We have lived in this place for a long time, a very long time, since the time when the world did not have this shape. We learned from the ancients that we are a tiny part of this immense universe, fellow travellers with all the animals, the plants and the waters. We are all a part of the whole, we cannot neglect or destroy our home. And now we want to talk to those who cannot yet manage to see the world in this way, to say to them that together we have to take care of the boat in which we are all sailing. . .'

If a terrestrial being can speak like this, I thought, he must have sprung from that world I was searching for. His name was Ailton, he was a Krenak Indian and, like most Indians today, he had added his tribal name to his Western name. He was the spokesman of the primeval forest and its people, of the world which I intended to enter, where I knew lay the rewards of my quest. Ailton Krenak, the magician, the little dark-haired Indian with burning black eyes and a dazzling smile, who nailed you to the wall with his piercing gaze; whose voice was soft and gentle and whose power was difficult to combat. I had met him only briefly at a soirée in his honour. He had seen my work on Africa and when I told him that I intended to attempt the same 'ouvrage' on the Indians of the Amazon, he smiled and softly said, 'We would be very honoured.' He fixed his eyes on me for a moment as if to underline his statement and then gently moved on through the many faces seeking his attention.

Before returning to Brazil he sent me a message. 'Tell Mirella', it said, 'that we are happy to receive her. *She will fall into the arms of the forest people who will carry her through the Amazon.*' With that message all my fears and apprehensions disappeared. The red light turned to green and within a week I had got myself into gear. I bought my camping equipment and a Varig air ticket to São Paulo and contacted my sponsors. It all happened so fast I did not stop to think what lay ahead. I just let myself float, drawn by some irresistible force, as if I were being sucked towards a destination over which I had no control. Ailton's quiet, powerful presence accompanied me. I remained uncharacteristically calm and just moved forward as if in a daze. It was a strange sensation and one I cannot explain.

So who is Ailton Krenak?

A charismatic Indian in his late thirties, Ailton Krenak is the National Co-ordinator of the Union of Indian Nations, President of the Forest Peoples' Alliance and Co-ordinator of the Indian programme of São Paulo radio, which reaches a large number of nations through Brazilian radio networks. He comes from the small tribe of Krenak Indians who in the 1920s were estimated to number 5,000, roaming an area of some 200 square miles. A census today reports 150 individuals living in fifteen square miles of land largely shared with encroaching ranchers. Having lived in the city for nearly twenty years he learned to read and write, and his strength of personality coupled with his experience of journalism and public relations have made him a powerful figure – catalyst, co-ordinator and charismatic leader of the forest peoples.

He told me of his childhood and upbringing. He was born in 1953 in the state of Minas Gerais, where the forest was by then already devastated and there were few animals and fish to hunt. His childhood was spent in an area that was being quickly settled, and in less than a decade the whole region was colonized and small villages and cities were being built. Today great industries are established there: steel works, paper factories and forestry enterprises.

At the age of seventeen he was encouraged by his grandfather and his family to migrate to a place where children could go to school, and the large tightly-knit family structure was dispersed. 'I still don't feel at home in São Paulo; I came here against my will, but in our tradition young people follow their family groups,' he says. At the end of 1970 he returned with some of his people to Minas Gerais. He had started to develop a broader awareness and began to realize that many other Indian groups like his own existed. He began to understand better the causes of their migration, why they were expelled from their territories and forced to go to foreign areas. He began to see the importance of working to preserve their regions, to protect the people and the traditional territories, and he started to make choices.

His first choice was to walk. He walked from the north to the south of Brazil, from the borders with Argentina to the Makuxi and Wapixana villages on the border of Venezuela, from the Indian villages on the coast of Bahia to those on the western borders with Bolivia, Peru and Colombia.

> 'This period was a time of understanding, finding out about the diversity of our country. It was the time when I began to understand the complexity of the world we live in and to learn about it. It was a very intense period

of my life. I walked with many Indians, relatives of many nations, and we formed a group of people pursuing a vision for the future of our people. By the end of 1970 those of my family who had remained in the forest had been reduced to about 200 people. Many died in the wars to defend their territories, which are now too small to support our traditional nomadic way of life.

> 'At this time I had to make an important choice. I had to decide whether to use my knowledge and experience to help my people secure our territory and the economic base of our land. It was then that I understood I have a great responsibility, because the world is for me today what my village was for me as a child.'

In 1979 the Union of Indian Nations (UNI) was set up to unite the councils of nearly 180 of Brazil's Indian nations, because white people were invading the Indian territories and threatening the balance of those regions. 'The greatest part of our work is in putting into practice the dreams of our elders, to cure nature, regenerate our regions, maintain the balance of culture and keep our spirit in balance with the universe. . . .' Ailton Krenak became the National Co-ordinator of the Union of Indian Nations and was elected President of the Forest People's Alliance in 1989.

> 'If we can build in the heart of the people of the city a beautiful forest made of friendship, music and celebration, then we can pacify their spirit so they can live with the people of the forest. This is our message . . .'

The drive from São Paulo airport to a friend's house displayed the ugly scars of uncaring human avarice and greed. A concrete jungle rose around us through a thick smog that stung our eyes and blurred our vision. My friend Charlò, with his sunny disposition, was the only ray of light. I clung to it like a beacon in the night.

And then Ailton reappeared to reassure me. Everything was going to be all right. His world within the ugly world we had temporarily re-entered was my final destination and he would lead me to it. I was, after all, an intrepid traveller heading towards the unknown environment from which he came. All I had to do was follow.

He received us graciously at his Union of Indian Nations headquarters two days later, and our meeting was bathed in the same betwitching aura of our first encounter. We sat with him on woven straw mats shaped like lotus leaves, which he spread on the ground beneath an ancient tree in the compound, and he talked for an hour. His full attention was upon us and he seemed well pleased with our exchange of views. But the language barrier stood between us like a wall of stone, and having to talk to him through an interpreter was another

frustration I had not reckoned with. I chose my words carefully so as not to offend his sensibility; experience in my past quests to record vanishing tribes across the world had taught me to tread carefully. Misinterpretations can cause a negative response. It was imperative that he should fully comprehend what I was seeking if he was to help me in my search. I found it difficult to gauge my words to his understanding. I turned the pages of my book on Africa to illustrate my points.

When finally the interview was over he shook my hand and said, 'Welcome to our struggle, your work will be important for us.' He moved away quietly and left us with his friend, another powerful-looking Indian from the Kaxinawa tribe. It was a good beginning, although still inconclusive. We would have to meet again, and perhaps again and again before we could begin. This was the rhythm we would now have to adopt. I had been warned of this and Ailton had expressly requested that I alter my occidental rhythm to that of the Indians if we were to work harmoniously together. Harmony was the crucial determining factor I would have to abide by. Somewhere along the line I would have to change gear again, slow down, reconstitute my rhythm to fit in with theirs. This was, I knew, going to be the single most difficult element I would have to deal with, but it was essential.

Before leaving London I had been approached by a BBC programme maker who proposed I record a diary of my quest. Ailton would, of course, play an important role in my film, for on him hung the whole infrastructure of my delicate operation. Or so I was led to believe. I could not wait to focus my camera lens on his face, to try and capture those fleeting, intangible elements that had so enraptured me. It was my first moving picture venture and a month of BBC training in London had got me well and truly hooked on this new medium. I asked Ailton for another appointment, an hour at the most.

We spent four hours together beneath the same ancient tree. My carefully prepared interview got completely out of hand when Ailton began to talk. He had a way with words; he strung them together like beads in a rare necklace, wielding and coaxing them so that simple sentences sounded like poetry. His answers to my questions took on dimensions way beyond my wildest expectations. He led us on a journey of discovery that orbited into outer space to the remote reaches of creation, where men and spirits convened in complete harmony with the earth; an extraordinary and simple exposé of life which defied all and any definitions I had ever heard. He spoke quietly, unhesitating, never searching for a word, as if he was in a trance, pausing whenever necessary to slow for translation. I had called on Laymert, a Brazilian friend and colleague of Ailton's who spoke perfect English, to join in our

sessions. What a godsend he was. I lost all track of time as my lens explored the fleeting shadows of emotion that moved across Ailton's face, the dark eyes, the thick black hair that fringed his face and fell to his shoulders.

Let me remind my readers at this point that I am a stills photographer, and now my images were moving. I was suddenly in control of a whole new dimension that allowed me to probe into the emotions of the soul and the mind, without forcibly having to freeze them. Heady stuff for a debutante. Ailton seemed in no hurry, he flowed on quietly, who knows, perhaps even enjoying the exchange. I did not wish to break the spell, my concentration was intense and then, just as suddenly as it had all started, it was over. Ailton stopped talking and fell silent for a long moment, staring into space, an expression of infinite sadness shrouding his expression. Four hours had slipped by, during which time I tried to touch on every possible feature essential to my work. I needed to enter his world; what better way than through his mind? We broke for lunch and then left each other, and I returned to the ugly, noisy, smelly world from which he had temporarily transported me.

The encounter left me feeling a little bit dizzy. I was much reassured, but still no sign of a concrete plan of action had appeared. I was perplexed, but decided to remain calm. I was after all changing rhythm. Not wanting to impose too heavily, I stayed away for a while. Ailton was a busy man under pressure, dealing with issues far more important than my own. I decided to wait for a signal. He was now aware of my presence, my aspirations and my needs. He would need time, I thought, to digest it and come up with some plausible programme for me to follow.

But the signal never came. I waited three weeks and then called his secretary for an appointment. I kept thinking of his response when asked how long it would take me to complete my work. 'It will take as long as is necessary, she will return when she has finished. . .'

I had noticed that if I stayed away from Ailton for long the reassurance he always managed to inject began to waver and I invariably became nervous, frustrated and insecure again. Our third and last meeting was baffling. Using every diplomatic ploy at my command, I gently but firmly told him that I felt it was now time to make some sort of plan. I had prepared a list of possible Indian nations that interested me, gleaned from the many images that had caught my eye. I explained clearly to him the reasons for my interest and again drew on my African book. He listened intently, fixing me with his fiery eyes, and said nothing. Silence fell between us. I held his gaze and waited for his response.

'It is possible that I have completely misunderstood you all this time? I had been planning to send you to find a tribe that has not yet made contact with the outside world, but you will need much time. No one can say how long it will take you to make contact and even if you will see them at all. You might just catch fleeting glimpses of them. It could take up to a year. . .'

'But Ailton,' I gasped, 'I'm a photogapher not an anthropologist. In order to get these sort of pictures I must not only be able to *see* them, but I need to see them well and get to know them so as to gain their confidence.' He smiled and gently said, 'Well then, that's not for you.' Now we were back to square one, and only now, after all these hours of talking, thinking that he was there with me on the same wavelength, did I realize that we were miles apart. I felt suddenly tense. Sensing my unease, he spoke reassuringly and then added, 'We'll have to think again. . .' Back to the drawing board we went. I pulled out all my research papers and tried to take hold of the situation. 'Let's take one tribe at a time from my list and you tell me how you feel about my visiting them. The Kampa, for instance: I was told they are among the most beautiful of the remaining tribes in Brazil, living much as they always have, way over on the Peruvian border. I could start with them.' 'OK,' he said, 'I'll arrange it and I'll call you tomorrow.' Two days later Ailton's secretary called. 'Ailton has fixed everything for you, Mirella. He has called a friend in Cruzeiro do Sul who will look after you and guide you to the Kampa. Everthing has been arranged, you can leave tomorrow, we'll organize the air tickets for you.' Four weeks after we had touched down in São Paulo we took off for the interior.

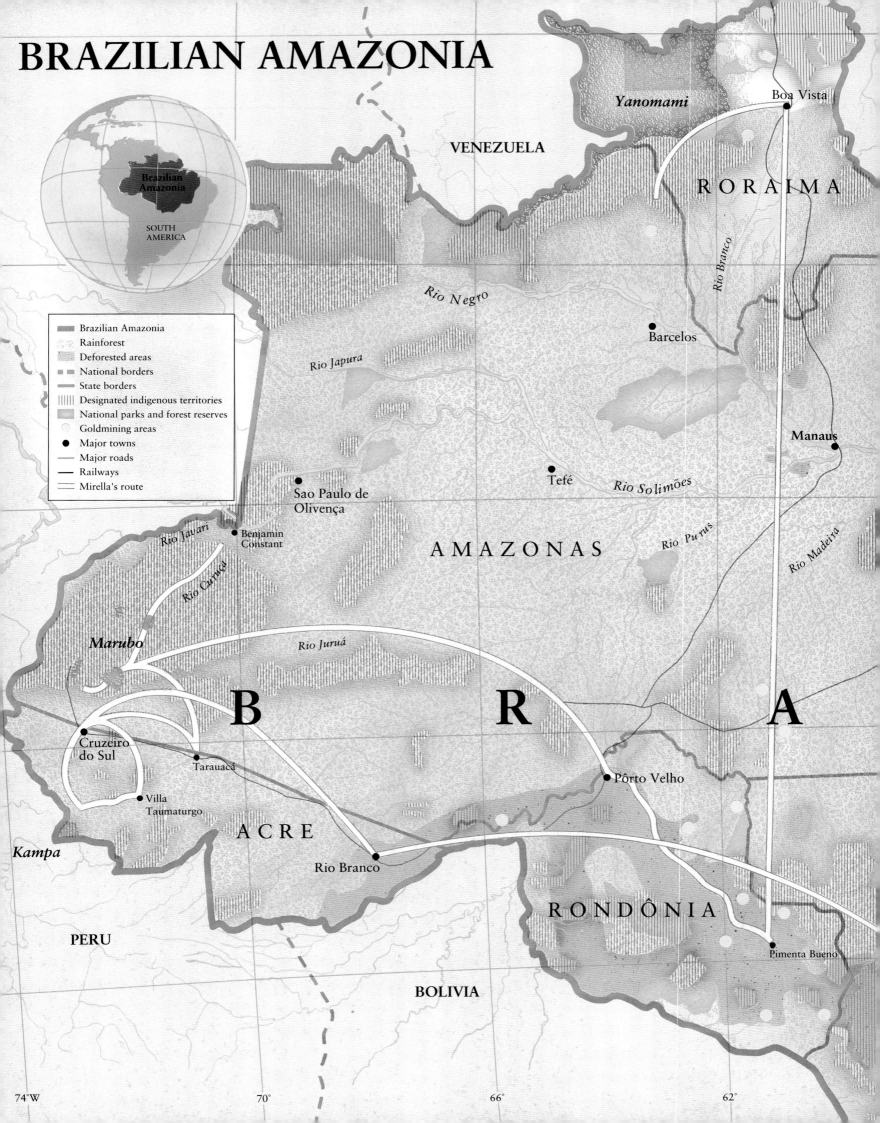

BRAZILIAN AMAZONIA

SOUTH
AMERICA

Brazilian
Amazonia

Brazilian Amazonia
Rainforest
Deforested areas
National borders
State borders
Designated indigenous territories
National parks and forest reserves
Goldmining areas
● Major towns
Major roads
Railways
Mirella's route

VENEZUELA

Yanomami

Boa Vista

R O R A I M A

Rio Negro

Rio Branco

● Barcelos

Rio Japura

Manaus

● Tefé

Rio Solimões

Sao Paulo de
Olivença

Rio Javari

● Benjamin
Constant

Rio Curuça

A M A Z O N A S

Rio Purus

Rio Madeira

Marubo

Rio Juruá

B

R

A

● Cruzeiro
do Sul

● Tarauacá

● Pôrto Velho

Kampa

● Villa
Taumaturgo

A C R E

Rio Branco

R O N D Ô N I A

PERU

Pimenta Bueno

BOLIVIA

74°W

70°

66°

62°

SURINAM

FRENCH
GUIANA

UYANA

JYANA

ATLANTIC

OCEAN

4°N

AMAPA

Brazilian Amazonia and Europe
shown to the same scale

Rio Trombetas

Rio Jari

Macapá ●

Brazilian Amazonia

0

Rio Amazonas

Belém ●

Monte
Alegre ●

Rio Amazonas

Cametá ●

São Luís ●

io Amazonas

Santarém ●

tacoatiara ●

MARANHÃO

PARÁ

Rio Irim

Rio Xingu

Rio Gurupi

4°S

Z

I

L

Rio Tapajos

Rio Tocantins

Carolina ●

PIAUÏ

Rio Araguaia

8°

GOIAS

MATO
GROSSO

12°

Rio das Mortes

Rio Parnaíba

from São Paulo

58°

54°

50°

46° W

FOREST PEOPLES OF THE AMAZON

ORIGINS

Long, long ago the ancestors did not exist. There was only Omao, the ancestral hero, and his brother Soawe. It was Omao who created us human beings, and the enemy Indians to the south and the foreigners. All these Omao created. It was us Indians that he was just about to create.

Down by the great river, Umao went to collect a hardwood tree, the slender *poli* tree that peels its smooth bark. He went on downstream, far downriver, to find it. When he returned to his house with the tree trunk, he said to his younger brother Soawe, who was lying in his hammock: 'Go and collect me more human beings!', then he went off to collect more himself.

Soawe lay in his hammock. 'Oh!' he thought after a while, 'My brother will expect me to work quickly to collect this wood, I'm afraid'. So he went out and hastily cut many lengths of softwood. Omao returned and saw all the softwood lying on the ground.

'That bad younger brother of mine has made me really angry,' said Omao. 'It was snakes that I was going to make all feeble, and it was human beings that I was going to make from the '*poli*' tree so that they could cast their skins. Once they had become really elderly, a man and his wife could have dived in the river and stripped off their skins, and become beautiful again.'

But instead Soawe had collected a load of rubbish and Omao became angry and made us humans from that. So it is that we human beings die really quickly. We were created from that rubbish. So we became weak. So we die. So we mourn, instead of being able to peel off our skins when we become really old, as we would like.

Myth, which provides the explanation for the origin of all things, underpins the societies of the Amazon. The myths describe a visionary world, through a rich imagery of nature, where the characteristics of plants and animals are explained and linked to human frailty, and behaviour. In myth, indeed, the animals are created from human ancestors and the behaviour of their human prototypes reflects the Indians' acute observation of animal behaviour.

In Indian belief the spirits which shaped the world and gave it meaning are still active. For behind the physical world that we all see the Indians perceive the continued working of these same forces. These energies can be seen in the play of light on water, the shining of seed down as it floats down from the canopy, the drip of moisture falling from puddles trapped in the great branches of the forest trees.

Dreaming provides ready but uncontrolled access to this realm and reveals the spirits' activities. Dreams warn of visitors approaching the isolated villages, provide news of wild pig nearby in the forests and reveal illness caused by the vengeful spirits of animals eaten by the community.

For the Indians know that whenever they kill animals or take produce from the forest they incur a debt. Natural forces, they say, are 'expensive'. They seek repayment. Eating meat in particular, while necessary to life, is dangerous. The Indians become charged with blood, 'smelly' and easily perceived by the ghosts of the dead animals, which seek revenge. Elaborate precautions must be taken to minimize this risk. Meat must be well cooked to drive out the smell and the blood. Some meats must be avoided by certain age groups. Women who are menstruating and their husbands, and men who have recently killed enemies are considered to be particularly at risk. They are already charged with blood and cannot risk consuming more. Hunters often do not consume the meat of animals that they themselves have killed.

The Indians' social world is ordered by their relations with the natural world that surrounds them.

Shamans and the cosmos

Most illness, the Indians believe, is caused by vengeful animal spirits. As one Indian explains: 'Your wife is menstruating. You kill a peccary. You eat the peccary. Then it is night. You dream. You see peccaries rooting on the ground, snuffle! snuffle! snuffle! Those dream peccaries are the evil spirits of the peccary. You hurt all over. Your guts begin to ache. You are infested with the worms that the peccaries eat. You get pains in your legs and back. You may die.'

Shamans are the Indians' spiritual specialists. It is they who learn to move at will in this spirit world, to control the forces of nature and restore health. They gain access to the spirit world by using powerful hallucinogenic drugs from infusions and snuffs made from a wide variety of barks, leaves, resins and seeds.

The colourful visions induced by these drugs are direct expressions of spiritual force. Young shamans must learn to control these experiences, recruiting the master spirits of the animals as their allies in the struggle against the spirits that cause disease. The Yanomami say that the shaman's body is like a house. The ribs of the chest are like rafters and the arms and legs like corner posts. The spirit allies must be brought in to populate the house.

At initiation, the young shaman is given massive doses of snuff. As one recalls:

> After I had taken a lot of snuff, I started to chant. The ground became red and flattened; beautiful. They sky began to sing *we! we! we!* The colours of the rainbow began to appear and swirl about like a snake. Then the spirit allies began to arrive. They were dancing as for a festival, their bodies all painted up. The toucan spirits arrived with their big ear sticks and bright red loin cloths. The hummingbird people arrived and flew around the place. My soul began to shine. One by one the spirits arrived, the *moka* frog spirits with quivers of arrows on their backs, the peccary spirits, the bat people, all the animal spirits came, the spirits of waterfall and fish spirits. All came and slung their hammocks in my chest.

These first experiences of the spirits' world are dangerous and insecure. The spirits may leave at any time and the young shaman has difficulty in controlling their force. It may be many years before he is trusted to cure the sick.

A headman of the Bororo tribe, photographed at the end of the nineteenth century. Traditionally the Indians of Amazonia, with the exception of the Kampa, have always gone virtually naked. On ceremonial occasions, however, the men in particular wear elaborate headdresses and body decorations.

The battle of the spirits

Curing is perceived by the Indians as a battle. The vengeful ghosts of dead animals in the soul of the sick person must be driven out by the more powerful master spirits recruited by the shaman. The spirits in the shamans' chests reveal themselves through their chants. In contrast to the often bellicose imagery of curing, the chants of the spirit allies are expressed in a different kind of poetry. The spirits playfully reveal themselves in an often comic manner, while their power is manifested in the light which shines from them.

> Arching, arching,
> The anaconda essence
> Arches downstream.
> The seed down falls
> Shining down, shining down.
>
> Down the river of little gourds
> The anahinga people are flirting.
> The anahinga man sticks foam
> On the anahinga girl,
> As they sail down the great river,
> In midstream, in midstream.

The shaman's access to the spirit world also give him other powers – to see into the future, to experience events far away. The master animal spirits who are allies also give him control over natural forces – to cause rain and storms, to attract game into nearby hunting grounds, to bring illness and death to his enemies.

The cycle of souls

Humans have their own spirits. Indeed, according to the Yanomami, each individual has a number of souls. A core soul forms from the father's sperm inside each foetus, and this core being lodges in the individual's chest, in his heart and blood. The throb of the heart and the rise and fall of the chest in breathing are signs that the human spirit is still there. At the same time each male child has a second soul born as a harpy eagle, while the 'reflections' of female children are weasels. The death of either of these animals inevitably causes the death of the human to which they are linked. Their hunting is thus proscribed. The core spirits are only weakly attached to young humans. They may be lured out of the body by forest beings, causing the human to weaken and die, unless the shamans are able to bring them back. Young children are closely tied to their parents, who have to observe strict taboos to ensure their children do not sicken. Many foods are prohibited to them and they must avoid sex for many months to avoid harm coming to their child. Only gradually does the child gain independence of the parents' spiritual guardianship. As the child's awareness grows, its spirit becomes more secure in its body.

But the approach of puberty brings another period of danger. Girls, in particular, are conceived as becoming highly charged with blood and attractive to vengeful forest spirits. As their first menses approach they are likened to clouds

Dugout canoes remain the principal mode of transport along Amazonia's vast network of rivers.

heavy with rain and many foods are prohibited to them. At menarche they are secluded from society and denied all but the blandest food, until, after having their hair shorn and being adorned with body paint, birds' feathers and cotton bandoliers, they are brought proudly back into the community to take their place in the adult world.

At death the core spirit becomes 'shifty'. Its attachment to the body weakens. It becomes discontented and moves gradually into the realm of the ghosts. The ghosts come to the dying human, they strum on the hammock strings in which he is lying. They lure the soul away. 'Come, come with us, you are my husband!', 'Come take my daughter!' they call out to the spirit. The core being prepares to leave. It takes down its arrows from the rafters. It makes itself a new liana hammock ready for the journey and leaves. The humans cry and call to the spirit to stay with them, stressing their kinship and shared life with the dying person. But the spirit leaves. Only the 'empty thing', the body, remains.

Smoking meat, probably wild pig. The Indians recognize the need to supplement their diet with animal protein, but at the same time are reluctant to eat too much meat. Hunter rarely eat their own prey, for fear that the animal's spirit will return to take revenge.

Shared lives

The lives of Amazonian Indians are ordered primarily by their ties with their kin. Their societies are intensely egalitarian. 'Chiefs', where they exist, have little power over others. Controls against misbehaviour are essentially informal, and are either negotiated between individuals or resolved by the consensus of the community. In some communities disputes are resolved through duelling, in which the miscreant and his challenger exchange an even number of blows. The leaders in Indian society are followed by others only so long as they are respected and their leadership is needed. On the contrary, children are brought up to be strongly individualist, to assert their own claims and feelings, to express openly their emotions and desires, and to defend themselves tenaciously and exact revenge for any and every infringement of their rights. Correspondingly, the Indians are imbued from their earliest years with a deep sense of the need to exchange and share. The primary and, in a sense only, immoral act in Amazonian life is selfishness. Personal property is very limited and goods move freely through the societies, creating a web of mutual obligations. All food is shared to all around the same hearth and meats are shared more widely to embrace all the community, thus ensuring a shared and adequate diet. To eat while others go hungry is to break your ties with society and invite contempt.

Long ago human beings did not have fire. They ate their food raw. It was Alligator who first had fire. He kept it hidden in his mouth.

He would go out collecting caterpillars with the Marbled Wood-quail People. In the forest, Alligator would light a fire and cook up his caterpillars. Then he would wrap the caterpillars again in fresh leaves and return to the village. When they exchanged food on return, Alligator passed on the uncooked caterpillars that the others gave him, while keeping the cooked ones for himself.

One day while the adults were out collecting caterpillars, Alligator's and Marbled Wood-quail's sons were playing. Little Marbled Wood-quail was scratching about on the floor and he found a cinder. When his father returned he showed it to him. So they knew that Alligator had fire. They decided to have a festival to make Alligator laugh. . . . Everyone laughed and Alligator laughed too. His mouth opened right up and he gave a huge guffaw.

'Ha ha ha ha!' he laughed, and as he did so, Tree Creeper snatched the fire and flew off . . . then Long-tailed Tyrant grabbed it. With the fire in his mouth, he flew right up high into the top of *coussapoa* tree.

'*Mai mai mai pio!*' sang Long-tailed Tyrant. The birds' tails had been burned by the fire. That is how fire got into that tree, which we use for making firesticks.

Frog cursed the animal ancestors who had stolen the fire.

'So keep this fire! You will sleep close to it for warmth but your children will die! You will burn your children in it when they die! You will grieve when this fire makes their eyes burst!' Frog and Alligator threw themselves into the river and remained in the cold.

Most Amazonian Indians have a very open and matter-of-fact approach to sex. Sex is understood as fundamental and integral to life, as perfectly normal while at the same time powerful, and therefore spiritually risky. Because of this element of risk, sex is proscribed to those being initiated into adulthood and as shamans, and to women and their husbands during menstruation. Husband and wife are also proscribed from having sex when their children are very young or ill.

Sex is considered as essentially a private matter, but privacy is viewed differently in Amazonian society. The dark of the communal hut may be considered seclusion enough for married couples, but in general most people prefer the greater privacy of the forests, where illicit liaisons are also consummated. While sex is a subject for jest and mockery, it is not a source of shame or fear. Most sex takes place in the context of marriage, but extra-marital affairs are also common and the subject of much gossip and ribaldry.

Making a living

The diffusion of power in Indian society is an important aspect of the Indians' adaptation to their environment. It means that large villages are unstable and frequently break up into smaller, widely separated communities. This reduces the pressure on the local environment which is crucial to the Indians' livelihoods.

For the Indians rely entirely on the jungle and their gardens for their welfare. It is a vigorous life made easy by their astonishing familiarity with their environment. The poor leached soils of the tropical forest cannot sustain permanent agriculture. Indian agriculture is accordingly undemanding on the soils. Gardens are cleared with axes in old-growth forest and, after being allowed to dry in the sun, the felled timber is burned. Most nutrients are lost in the burn and the rains, but the ashes give a temporary fertility to the soil. Yams, sweet potatoes, bananas, plantains, cocoyams and cassava form the staples and are the main crops among the sixty or so species that the Indians cultivate. Such crops have been selected because they are undemanding and grow easily in the nitrogen-poor soils, providing the Indians with a dependable source of calories. But the nitrogen-poverty of the soils is reflected in the protein content of the crops, which is also very low. Consequently the Indians rely on hunting, fishing and gathering to provide the protein and mineral supplements essential to a balanced diet.

The fact that both kinds of foods are essential to a proper diet is fully recognized by the Yanomami, who have two separate words for hunger: *ohi* – hunger pure and simple, and – *naiki* – hunger for protein. While satisfying *ohi* is just a matter of gardening, satisfying *naiki* is a challenge and an adventure. The Indians are superlative hunters.

The Indians hunt traditionally with longbows, using arrows made from canes grown in their gardens. In some areas blowpipes are the main weapon. All hunting is carried out by men, mostly alone or in pairs. Game is tracked, stalked and shot with great stealth and cunning, the hunter relying on his agility and ability to read the spoor and interpret animal noises to lead him to his prey. Hunters can recognize the calls of virtually all animal species and can mimic their calls to attract them. They can identify the tracks of all the larger game and, by carefully reading the ground, can even tell how long ago animals passed by, at what speed and with what probable goal. Most game consists of larger birds, monkeys and rodents, like agouti and paca. Larger animals like tapir, peccaries (wild pigs) and deer are hunted collectively or with dogs.

Some Indian societies are closely associated with the rivers. Fishing may be important to their lives and the villages are often large and stable, and agriculture well developed. Other communities live in the uplands and in forests between the major rivers. For them making a living is a more mobile affair, with long periods when they abandon their gardens and trek in the forests, setting up temporary shelters well away from their normal hunting grounds.

Apart from hunted game the forest provides the Indians with a wealth of other products: honey, fruits, crustaceans, edible caterpillars and other small animals like frogs, which are collected by hand, often by women. Besides this the forest provides rope, thatch, all building materials, dyes and poisons, which in turn are used for hunting and fishing. The Indians also use the forest as a source for the drugs which they use to penetrate into the realm of the spirits.

Yet the Indians' life is an easy one. To carry out all their chores – hunt, gather, garden, fish, collect firewood, cook and accomplish other domestic tasks – they work little more than forty hours a week. The rest of their time is their leisure, which they devote to raising their children, to gossip and discourse, to ritual and sleeping. It is a way of living with nature that westerners find hard to understand.

As the Amarakaeri of eastern Peru explain:

> We Indians were born, work, live and die in the basin of the Madre de Dios river of Peru. It is our land – the only thing we have, with its plants, animals and small farms: an environment we understand and use well. We are not like those from outside who want to clear everything away, destroying the richness and leaving the forest ruined forever. We respect the forest; we make it produce for us.
>
> Many people ask why we want so much land. They think we do not work all of it. But we work it differently from them, conserving it so that it will continue to produce for our children and our grandchildren. Although some people want to take it from us, they destroy and abandon it, moving on elsewhere. But we cannot do that; we were born in our woodlands. Without them we will die.
>
> In contrast to other parts of the Peruvian jungle, Madre de Dios is still relatively sparsely populated. The woodlands are extensive, the soils poor,

Indians display tremendous skill in deploying their traditional weapons, managing with ease to spear fish using longbows and arrows. They sometimes also paralyse or asphyxiate the fish by putting drugs derived from forest plants in the water.

so we work differently from those in other areas with greater populations, less woodland and more fertile soils. Our systems do not work without large expanses of land.

VICTIMS

When westerners first came to Brazil there were as many as ten million Indians living in Amazonia, more than half of whom were in Brazil. Today in Brazilian Amazonia only some 200,000 of these people remain. Sailing down the Amazon from the Peruvian highlands, in their half-crazed search for gold, the first Spanish explorers noted that the banks of the Amazon were almost continously populated. As archaeologists have now revealed, here, along the fish-rich river, lived complex and hierarchical societies, with expressive earthenware pottery, rich fruit groves and tanks of domesticated turtles. Yet today the banks of the Amazon are scarcely inhabited by Indians, as they have been swept away by enslavement and disease.

Early explorers were overwhelmed by the richness and profusion of the rainforest, as can be seen from engravings such as this illustration to von Spix and Martius's *Travels in Brazil in the years 1817–24*.

Brazil took its name from the word *brasile*, which the country's first visitors from the Old World gave to the wood that they felled to produce a dye for the fashionable courtiers of Europe. From the start the traders were reliant on the labour of the Indians to move the great logs to the coasts. As one observed, 'The only profit that these poor people derive from so much effort might be some miserable shirt or the linings from some clothing of little value. . . . After they have carried the logs to the ships during several journeys, you see their shoulders all bruised and torn by the weight of the wood – which is well known to be heavy and massive. This is hardly surprising, since they are naked and carry these loads so far.'

'King sugar'

As it had begun so it continued. The assault began in earnest in the seventeenth century with the growing demand for labour in the sugar plantations on the Brazilian coast. Slaving expeditions, rowed upriver by Indian slaves, fell on the small communities to take their able-bodied members down to the coast. The assaults were frequently assisted by missionaries, who were engaged in a process of forcing Indians to abandon their forest villages and dwell in centralized *reducciones* under close mission control.

By 1650, the Vice General of the Portuguese colony of Maranahão claimed that in the first decades since their arrival in the area the Portuguese had killed almost two million Indians, destroyed 'in their violent labour, exhausting discoveries, and unjust wars'. By the turn of the century the lower rivers were almost completely depopulated and it was necessary to go two months upriver, as far as the lands of the Omagua Indians near the present day Colombian border, to find any slaves. Although the sugar mills were eventually supplied with labour from Africa, slaving continued in Amazonia until the mid-nineteenth century. It boomed anew during the rubber era, when the discovery of the process of vulcanizing rubber turned the soft latex derived from the region's wild rubber trees into a valuable commodity, for which the industrial market in the north had an unquenchable demand.

For a time, the Amazon experienced unprecedented affluence – for a few. Dependent on the local Indians as a work force to tap the latex from the widely dispersed trees in the forests, the rubber traders resorted to every form of trickery and violence to ensure a supply of the precious fluid. Although actual slavery was well documented during the era, the more usual practice entailed a system of debt-peonage, still common in parts of Amazonia, whereby the Indian became trapped by his debts into working for a single *patrão*, who made his living, often a good one, from his position as entrepreneur.

A new El Dorado

The systematic exploitation of the Amazon region by outside interests continues today with all the power of modern technology. In the mid-1960s Brazil's military government opened up the country to foreign investment by offering tempting fiscal incentives to overseas capital. By 1966 the government itself, emboldened by the initial success of its much-vaunted 'Economic Miracle', began a massive investment in the region under the title of 'Operation Amazon', which in turn developed into the 'National Integration Plan' of the 1970s.

Vast road networks were slashed across the face of the forest, making the area accessible to big business and opening the lands to an invasion of ranchers, land speculators and impoverished settlers, while bringing disease and death to the region's remaining Indians. Entire tribes were blasted into extinction by the shock of contact, with single epidemics carrying off up to 30% of the population. It is estimated that one tribe a year has been lost in Brazil since the turn of the century. Settlers, fleeing landlessness and poverty, have flooded up these roads in their thousands, urged on by government slogans and offers of free land. Amazonia, a 'land without men for men without land', has become a great dumping ground for 'surplus people'.

The government has hailed the resettlement as a land reform. But land reform is just what it is not. In Brazil 70% of the rural population lacks land title, while 0.7% of farms occupy 43% of the land area. It is this concentration of land in the hands of the few, coupled with the mechanized farming of non-forested lands to produce cash crops for export, that has created land hunger. Rather than face the politically unsavoury task of redistributing non-forest lands, the government has opted for colonizing the rainforests.

The results have been ecological devastation on an enormous scale. In the state of Rondônia, where this process has been accelerated by World Bank funding, the 1960 population of 10,000 people, mainly Indians, boomed to over 1 million by 1985. Forest loss accelerated correspondingly, from 1,200 square kilometres in 1975 to over 16,000 by 1985. According to one estimate an area of rainforest the size of Great Britain would have been destroyed by 1990. Tragically, only 7% of the newly etablished settlements have proved successful.

The expectation that fertile soils underlie the lush forests has proved ill-founded. Quite unlike temperate ecosystems, where the soil is a major store of fertility, in tropical forests most plant nutrients are locked up in the living system. The nutrients are recycled from fallen bough and leaf direct to root and stem. Rapid decomposition in the hot, wet conditions quickly breaks down the fallen debris, and a web of fungal hyphae draws the released nutrients straight into the

The Indians are superlative hunters, yet never kill more than they need. Whether as hunters, gatherers or agriculturalists, they demonstrate an understanding of their environment which allows them to exploit it without damaging it.

shallow mat of roots. Remove the trees and the nutrients store is removed too, exposing a weak and vulnerable soil to the combined forces of torrential rain and tropical sun. The results are disappointing for the farmer, and disastrous for the soils. Deprived of its protective cover, the land becomes waste – huge expanses of coarse scrub, unusable grassland and lateritic hardpan.

Despite these disappointments, Amazonia remains for many an El Dorado concealing fabulous wealth – a vast reserve of natural resources to be exploited to promote Brazil's dizzy process of industrialization and pay off the country's US$120 billion debt. Already over two-thirds of Brazil's booming population live in the coastal cities, most in conditions of appalling squalor and deprivation – only forty years ago the figure was less than a quarter. The 'development' of Brazil's industrial base is now predicated on using Amazonia's natural wealth to secure the country's place in the international market.

In eastern Amazonia a government programme of regional development, costing some US$62 billion, is forging ahead, the aim being to turn an area the size of Britain and France combined into a giant agro-industrial park – the so-called Greater Carajas Programme. Iron ore from one of the world's largest mines, part-funded by the World Bank and the European community, trundles east down a 500-mile-long railway to a specially created port near the mouth of the Amazon. There the ore is exported to Europe at concessionary rates, negotiated when the loans were agreed to, 'to ensure the competitiveness of the European Steel Industry'.

Cheap steel has its price. The loans from the European Community and World Bank have also ensured the destruction of the region's Indians and forests. The fiscal incentives and tax holidays that are part of the Carajas development's economic logic have stimulated a number of Brazilian companies to set up pig-iron smelters all along the railway. With the cheap iron ore and transport provided by the mine, the smelters will make an easy untaxable profit for ten years, fuelled by charcoal cut from the local forests. According to the Forest Institute of Rio de Janeiro University, within seven years the smelters will consume 10% of Brazil's Amazonian forests.

Images of nature

The Indians are not victims solely of economic forces over which they have no control. They are also subject to the stereotypes and images imposed from outside. For if on the one hand westerners have appeared merciless in their exploitation of the Indians and their lands, they have also been amazed on the other hand by their nakedness and the absence of what they consider the essentials of civilization – as the French missionaries said, '*sans dieu, sans loi, sans roi*'. They have thus invested the Indians with their fantasies. The Indians have become a canvas on which westerners work out their notions of human nature – cannibals and devil-worshippers to some, nature's innocents and noble savages to others.

The process started with the first contact between the two worlds. As Christopher Colombus wrote to his king on first seeing Indians:

> They are very well built with fine bodies and handsome faces. Their hair is coarse almost like that of a horse's tail. . . . They are the colour of Canary Islanders (neither white nor black). . . . They love their neighbours as

Amazed by the Indians' nakedness and their lack of civilization, westerners have always tended to impose their own stereotypes on them, viewing them as noble savages, untamed cannibals, or lost souls ripe for conversion.

themselves and their way of speaking is the sweetest in the world, always gentle and smiling. . . . They are so affectionate and have so little greed and are in all ways so amenable . . . that there is in my opinion no better people and no better land in all the world.

For many, however, the Indians' nakedness and lack of civilization was at once an affront and challenge. Here were lost souls, peoples who had never heard of Christ, who had to be redeemed both with the Christian message and the learning of a superior civilization. As a Capuchin missionary wrote earlier this century:

The missionary knows how to accomplish at the same time the duties imposed on him as a priest, the legacy of Christ among the unbelievers, and as a colonist, the legacy of Government among savages. These duties mutually aid and complement each other, for to christianise without colonising or colonise without christianising is to plough in the sand or build castles in the air.

Many missionaries today have rejected this approach, and, in the words of the Jesuit Bartolomeu Melia realize that:

all they have done to help the Indian will have no other effect than to lay the ground for an invasion by neo-colonial peoples who will try to get rid of the Indians, either by eliminating them or by reducing them to marginal status. The map of the Americas is dotted with cities founded as missions in native territories where today the Indian is a stranger and a beggar.

With the help of a new theology of liberation many missionaries have now become some of the most effective champions of Indian rights. Yet fundamentalistic sects who see themselves as 'Commandos for Christ' continue to pursue isolated tribes who flee contact with the outside world, describing their goal as 'reaching the lost until we have reached the last'. Such missionaries genuinely believe that the Indians are doomed to perdition, that shamanism is devil worship, and that at death the Indians will be cast into eternal fires. They can be found in all corners of Amazonia today, relentlessly drilling Indians to reject Satan and choose eternal life.

Such negative images tie in well with those others who see the Indians as 'obstacles to progress', to be pushed aside to make way for development. Yet another stereotype, more subtly pernicious, has also proved a great stumbling block for the Indians. This is the image which sees the Indians as already perfect beings, innocent and childlike in the ways of the outside world, who must be preserved uncontaminated and protected from all contact. For such people, the Indians' desire for western goods – for fishhooks and machetes, clothes and transistor radios – is a sign of their fall from grace.

FIGHTING FOR A FUTURE

In fact, however, the Indians have never been passive in the face of change. They have resisted both the invasion of their lands and the violation of their rights, and have sought to accommodate themselves to the culture of the newcomers. In Brazil, the Indians were until 1988 denied the rights of full citizenship. They were considered legal minors, 'relatively incapable before the law'. As they were wards of the state, their own organizations were not recognized and the government negotiated on their behalf. Since this has effectively meant that they have been denied the legal and political means to redress their grievances, many Indians have continued to use arms to defend themselves.

A typical case concerns the northern Kayapo (Txukarramae) Indians of the Xingu river, whom the government wanted to relocate in the 1970s to an 'Indian Park' south of their lands. The Indians resisted the move and instead sought to defend their own land against encroaching cattle ranchers. In an Amazonian version of the wild west, the Txukarramae repeatedly attacked the ranches, killing over thirteen cowhands over a fifteen-year period and successfully preventing the takeover of their territory. Their leader during this period learned much of the western world, becoming the subject of a number of films. The lessons he learned of how to use the media to manipulate public opinion were to serve him well.

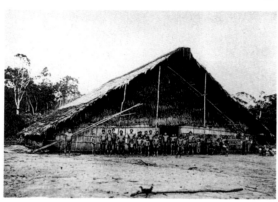

The *maloca*, or communal hut, is the focus of the Indians' life. Built with materials from the jungle, *malocas* are abandoned every few years, when the Indians move to another part of their lands and allow the jungle to reclaim their former dwelling.

Frustrated by the continuing failure of the government Indian agency to provide them with legal protection, in March 1984 the Indians decided on a course of direct confrontation with the government. Taking care to make the media aware of what was going on, they took hostage the non-Indian director of the Xingu Indian 'Park' along with five other members of the government's National Indian Foundation. The Indians refused to release their hostages until their legal rights were properly recognized.

Tension mounted to fever pitch as the military flooded the area with soldiers, while journalists and film crews converged for a replay of 'Wounded Knee'. The headlines warned of an impending act of 'genocide', and in the full glare of publicity the government was forced to give way: the Indians got their land.

Four years later, the same Indians raised the stakes, directly confronting plans to build a huge pair of dams that would have flooded them off their lands. The government plans were in fact nationwide, and included the building of 136 dams, 60 of which would flood Indian lands. When the plans were leaked to the public, it was learned that the Brazilian government was attempting to secure World Bank financing for this programme. The news provoked an international outcry from concerned human rights and environmental organizations such as Survival International and the Environment Defense Fund.

Press attention focused on the campaign to halt these loans after two Indians travelled to Washington to urge the World Bank not to finance the flooding of their lands. On their return to Brazil they found themselves charged under Brazil's 'law of foreigners' with 'denigrating the image of Brazil abroad'. In October 1988, the trial of one of the Kayapo, Kube'i, caused a national uproar when he arrived at the court house in traditional dress with 400 other Indians. The Kayapo were prevented from entering the court by the military police, while the judge refused to allow Kube'i into the courtroom until the Kayapo leader 'dressed in shirt and pants', for he considered the leader's attire 'a sign of disrespect' to the court. The judge did, however, uphold a decision to submit the two Kayapo leaders to psychological, anthropological and psychiatric tests 'to determine their level of acculturation and whether they were aware that they were committing a crime against Brazil'.

In defiance of this legislative farce, the other Kayapo leader, Bepkororoti Paiakan, travelled round Europe and Canada, visiting bankers and ministers of overseas development to put his case and to invite them to a meeting in February 1989 to listen to the Amazon people's voice. The meeting, which took place in the town of Altamira in the last week of February, secured global attention.

Hundreds of Indians representing some twenty different Amazonian Indian peoples assembled to demand the halting of dam projects that flood their lands. They demanded the right to be consulted about plans that will affect their futures and were joined by international environmental organizations that called for an end to the global financing of unsustainable development in Amazonia.

A quiet revolution

These spectacular methods of direct confrontation have attracted most international attention to the Indians' struggle. The Indians have purposefully exploited the sensationalism of the press and cannily played on western images of the Indians as plumed and naked defenders of nature. Yet over the last twenty years Amazonia has experienced a quieter but no less formidable development of Indian power.

The experiment can be traced back to Ecuador in the 1960s, where Shuar Indians faced with the gradual break-up of their lands on the agricultural frontier began to organize to confront the invasion. The Indians created a 'Federation of Shuar Centres' and embarked on a vigorous programme to gain land security and promote community development. Within twenty years land title had been gained for the majority of Shuar communities; they established their own radio station broadcasting in their own language and developed bilingual and bicultural education programmes. Primary health care programmes administered by the Indians were developed with state assistance.

The Shuar experience has been repeated with numerous variations all over Amazonia. Clusters of communities along the same river valleys have come together to form local cultural associations. Regionally they have grouped their new community-based organizations into federations, and national confederations. The majority of Amazonian Indian communities are now linked to these kinds of institutions.

Through their national-level confederation, they have even allied themselves internationally, so that today Amazonian Indians from Brazil, Bolivia, Peru, Ecuador and Colombia are internationally coordinated through their own secretariat. Indians regularly travel to the United Nations and the World Bank to negotiate for a recognition of their rights. They are involved in discussion with UN agencies on plans to halt tropical deforestation. Some of these institutions are now so well organized and respected that western governments are directly financing their work from their overseas development budgets.

Green alliances

The tragedy of Amazonia is that ever since 1500 it has been denied the chance of developing according to its own logic. Instead it has been subjected to forces from outside the forest, even outside the continent, controlled by people who know almost nothing about the region and care even less for the area's inhabitants. The

Indians have a different vision of the future. They look to a development based on the community, secure on its own lands. There, they believe, the ancient knowledge that they have drawn out of the forest over centuries can create a future based on a respect for human needs and nature's rhythm.

By westerners' standards, used as we are to permanent agriculture on the rich and stable soils of temperate climes, the Indians' extensive use of land appears wasteful, even profligate. But, as successive students of the region have pointed out, there are no 'western standards' for the successful occupation of Amazonia. All modern attempts to develop the Amazon have proved to be economic failures, ignorant of the weakness of the soils (to which the Indians' economies are so skilfully attuned), and based on political systems that have concentrated wealth outside the region rather than sharing it among those who have worked the land.

The Indian movement is now entering a crucial second phase. The Indian's successful and continued resistance to outside planning has proved the value of their newly achieved unity, and they are now aware that they need to go further, to align their struggle with other movements and create the basis for a genuine alternative. Inside the region they have found unexpected allies in the rubber tappers. After a century of enmity, Indians and tappers in Brazil have united in an Alliance of Forest Peoples to confront those who would fell the forests. While the Indians have fought successfully for a new place in the Brazilian constitution, which now gives them the status of full citenzenship and provides stronger guarantees to their lands, the rubber tappers have called for the creation of 'extractive reserves'. Some of these have now been created. Within them, freed from the debt-slavery they have endured for so long, the tappers aim to develop a new future based on the collection of forest products by rural cooperatives.

A *maloca* in its clearing. Indians clear small areas of the forest for their dwellings and 'gardens', but always move on before the land is exhausted.

Outside the region, the Indians have sought links with the non-governmental movements of the north. Human rights organizations in Europe and the United States have been effectively supporting the Indian cause since the 1970s. The Indians' novel organizations also received critical financial support from voluntary development agencies right through the 1980s. Now, in the 1990s, the Indians are strengthening their alliance with the western environmental movement. With the environmentalists' support they hope to project their vision of what 'development' really means for them. As the Indians note:

> Development can only occur when the people it affects participate in the design of proposed policies, and the model which is implemented thereby corresponds to the local peoples' aspirations. Development can be guaranteed only when the foundations are laid for the sustained wellbeing of the region; only continued poverty can be guaranteed when the policies lead to the pillage and destruction of local resources by those coming from outside. The indigenous people of the Amazon have always lived there: the Amazon is our home. We know its secrets well, both what it can offer us and what its limits are. For us, there can be no life if our forests are destroyed. We want to continue living in our homelands.

Opposite A Kampa girl wearing the traditional *kushma*.

Pages 32-3 Kampa children dwarfed by the giant buttresses of a felled rainforest tree.

By canoe to the Kampa

A five-hour flight with a two-hour time change landed us in Rio Branco in the state of Acre, one of the worst areas of devastation in Brazil. Half an hour before landing, the acrid smell of burning wood began to permeate the aircraft. I looked down to earth and saw the world on fire. A thick smoke haze hung ominously on the horizon like a shroud. Now and again great tongues of flame lashed skywards, punctuating the infernal scene with alarming exclamation marks. All the destruction we had read about or seen on film was now here beneath us in stark reality. For miles around ancient trees lay everywhere like a fallen army, charred and smouldering. It was a devastating sight that filled us with horror and alarm. The message of doom threatening the world was powerfully hammered home.

Ailton's friend, Macedo, was at the airport to meet us. Over the past ten years he had single-handedly created the first rubber tapper's co-operative, which helped to fend off the greedy rubber barons who had so ruthlessely and pitilessly exploited them for their own personal gain. He was familiar with the Kampa tribe and the area we were heading for, and was to find someone to look after us. That night we camped in hammocks on the wooden verandah of a friend of his; next day we left together with our seventeen pieces of luggage for the hour-long flight to Cruzeiro do Sul, near the Peruvian border.

In Cruzeiro the forest all around the airport was ablaze. A great wall of fire skirted the runway down which we taxied to a halt in front of the simple airport building.

We set up our mattresses and sleeping bags on the floor of the rubber tappers' headquarters, a simple wooden house on stilts on a hill overlooking the town. With Macedo's friendly help we began to trace our first route into the forest and we shopped for food and last-minute camping necessities. A week later we took off by air with Macedo's friend Achino for Villa Taumaturgo, a small village an hour's flight away by light aircraft. We landed on a strip that had been carved out of the forest beside the Amonia river, hired a canoe with an outboard motor and ventured into the interior.

Our first taste of jungle fever was bitter-sweet. Within twenty-four hours of our arrival our arms and legs were covered with nasty pink welts: we must have had at least five hundred each. The invisible inhabitants of the primeval forest had had a field day, and we quickly learned that in the Amazon the teeming insect life follows a hectic rhythm. Approximately every six hours a different variety emerges. Our 'delicate' skins, not yet hardened by the harsh climatic conditions, attracted them like nectar. They landed in droves, and we did not even notice them until the skin began to itch and swell about an hour later. By eight o'clock in the morning the heat and humidity of the forest began to rise and by noon it was ferocious. It was the end of the dry season and the river was it its lowest. Sandbanks, rocks and fallen trees littered the riverbed, and we had to negotiate a path between them.

The Brazilians, accustomed to this mode of travel, have devised an ingenious shaft for their outboard motors. About ten feet long, it stretches backwards at an angle of approximately thirty-five degrees. The propellor is attached to the end of this pole, and is just sufficiently immersed beneath the surface of the water to drive the long wooden canoe forward. Whenever an impediment appears the shaft and propellor are hoisted out of the water and long sturdy poles push the vessel around it. The boatmen are so accustomed to this mode of travel that they steer their craft with the dexterity of lorry drivers in difficult terrain.

I had had my first experience of river travel a few years before, when we crossed Africa from the Indian Ocean to the Atlantic on the rivers and lakes of the Equator. That had seemd to me like an adventure, but by comparison it was like travelling on a highway. At first I was alarmed, but the easy confidence of the boatmen's performance quickly reassured me, and the obstacle course drove the boredom from what could otherwise have been a monotonous journey. We travelled upstream for three days through magnificent jungle scenery, mooring at night along the riverbanks, where the rubber tappers lived in simple wooden shacks thatched with great leaves from the forest trees. Hospitable, warm and friendly, they welcomed us into their meagre accommodation and shared their food with us. It was a sort of undisputed cordiality that was extended quite naturally to all travellers through the jungle; a silent understanding of hardships shared. The families were always large, with never fewer than six children and sometimes as many as twelve or fourteen. I couldn't help wondering whether this apparent over-population might be one of the elements threatening the rainforest: with so many mouths to feed, the trees had to go to make room for edible crops and extra income. But it is not just pressure of numbers that is forcing settlers to push into the forest. And at the same time the Indian population of the rainforest is only about a tenth of what it was at the time of first contact by westerners.

Then we caught sight of our first Kampa on the river: a family of four – husband, wife and two small children – drifting towards us under the lush canopy, in a slender wooden canoe. From a distance it looked much like a log, clearing the water by only a few inches. They crouched like crows one behind the other, absolutely still and draped in their dark brown *kushmas*, the traditional handwoven dress. A small paddle guided their vessel over the water with barely a ripple. It was a rare, timeless vision, as if out of a dream. We waved at them as they passed; their chiselled faces framed by thick black hair stared back at us, expressionless at first, and then lit up by momentary smiles of greeting. We were nearing our destination.

We spent two wonderful weeks with the Kampa, during which we were slowly initiated into the lives of our first Amazonian Indians. It was an excellent beginning: we had broken the ice. I felt reassured, more confident and reconciled with my doubts. The beautiful Kampa were extraordinarily amenable to our needs, allowing us to move and work freely in their midst with never a harsh word or sign of intolerance. Our approach was gentle and respectful and in return we were received with friendly grace.

Our visit had been announced to their chief Antonio and his wife Dona Picci by radio from Cruzeiro do Sul. The whole family came out to meet us, ten of them in all, sons and daughters, grandchildren and friends. They led us to their home and helped us heave our luggage up the slippery riverbank. Drained as we were by the heat and the insects, and by the strain of our three-day river journey, our fatigue seemed to melt away in the warmth of their welcome.

We unpacked our bags for the first time since leaving London, and Dona Picci put an empty house in her compound at our disposal. It was a dream place, a wooden structure raised on stilts about eight feet above the ground, with a large thatched roof and no walls. We pitched our tents on the floorboards and set up camp, beautifully sheltered from the weather and the insects, with a view over the lush forest, the river and the Kampa banana plantations.

Antonio's son Francisco became our guide, and every morning we left with him in his motorized canoe to visit families up and down the river. He always went ahead and announced our arrival, explaining the reason of our visit to the head of the families, so that when we appeared they seemed quite impervious to our cameras.

The visual impact was extraordinary. I focused in on images so pure and timeless they belonged to another age. Working with these beautiful gentle people who so easily accepted our intrusion was a great bonus, for it allowed me to concentrate on the quality of my images and eliminated the anxieties usually associated with more tricky shooting conditions. I have rarely worked in such sympathetic conditions and could not believe my luck. My morale soared and my fears and hesitations left me. From now on it would be plain sailing, or so I thought.

For the Kampa, as for almost all the Indian tribes of the Amazon, manioc is the staple of their diet. The root may be processed in several different ways: dried and ground into flour, baked in hot ashes like a sweet potato, or turned into a sort of pitta bread which is cooked on a hot plate. It is also used to make a rather potent fermented beverage: the roots are boiled and then squashed into a creamy porridge-like mush with a wooden pestle and mortar. The fermenting agent is saliva. Mouthfuls of the mush are masticated until liquid and then spat out into a bowl. This is left in the sun until fermentation starts and then poured into the steaming porridge. The concoction is then covered with banana leaves and left to cool off for several hours. When the liquid has been strained through a small basket it is ready to drink. It was offered to me several times, but I could never bring myself to taste it. Somehow the notion of a spit-fermented beverage was beyond my spirit of adventure.

The Kampa introduced us to the ancient mystical Inca hallucinogenic beverage, *ayahuasca*. Curious for the experience, we asked Francisco to arrange a meeting with the *pagé*, the local medicine man, who lived alone with his mother several hours upstream from our camp. Another hour's walk through the dense forest on a little winding path led us to a clearing beside an arm of the river. Two small thatched wooden houses on stilts overlooked the water in a setting straight out of a children's story book. The sun was sinking when we arrived and the place was still and silent, bathed in the evening glow.

The *pagé* sat immobile as a wooden statue. He did not move at our approach, but just watched us advance through the smoke coiling from his pipe. Francisco spoke to him, explaining our wishes. He smiled mischievously and nodded at us.

Next day he went into the forest before first light and returned with an assortment of leaves and bark which he cut up and brewed for six hours in a cauldron over an open fire. The resulting dark brown liquid was solemnly served to us in a small round tin cup after nightfall, when the sky was hung with stars. We sat outside beside each other in solemn meditation for half an hour, facing a small table on which stood the bottle containing the magic potion and the cup. A small oil lamp flickered like a candle beside it. It looked like an altar. The cup was filled and then ceremoniously offered to each of us in turn. Imagining that it would probably taste awful, I stuffed a sweet into my trouser pocket, took a deep breath and threw the liquid back. It was like swallowing liquid quinine which burned my throat like acid. We settled down hunched on a log in the dark and waited. Nothing happened. After half an hour the *pagè* rose and silently passed the cup around again.

Our eyes became accustomed to the dark and we were soon able to discern the six Kampa silhouetted against the faint starlit sky. They crouched in a row like silent night owls, breathing heavily, spitting and burping, emitting strange gurgling sounds the like of which I had never heard. The scene took on a surreal aspect when they began hyperventilating and cooling off their perspiring bodies by flailing their heavy *kushmas* against their chests, producing sounds like great flapping wings.

The night chill seeped through my clothes, mosquitoes attacked my ankles and nothing happened. I was offered another dose and a little later left the group and stretched out on my inflatable mattress beneath my mosquito net and pulled the sleeping bag snugly around me. I might as well be comfortable if I was to enjoy the ride. I lay for a while picking out the constellations in the sky, and did not feel my body going numb and turn to stone. It suddenly weighed a hundred tons. My head was light as bubbling champagne. I closed my eyes and took off into the cosmos: great fountains of brightly coloured images began exploding like fireworks inside my head. They fell like sparks of fire, each with a precise shape and colour. I can still remember them quite vividly. There were precious stones – diamonds and emeralds, rubies and sapphires – and stars, leaves and flowers, exotic birds and butterflies, feathers and fish, and trees with fiery branches and curling roots beneath which sat a cheetah with a diamond collar and ruby eyes. The images kept coming, like a volcano erupting. It was a wild and beautiful sensation that lasted for five hours and then stopped, as I gently returned to earth and it was over. My body came back to life and my mind began to focus on things familiar. I heard the mosquitoes buzzing outside my net and recognized the stars in the sky. The sleeping bag was soft and warm. My travelling companions were still somewhere far away. They were now singing a haunting melody and humming a refrain that seemed to echo through the night. I lay and listened to them for a while and then fell into a deep sleep.

The honeymoon period ended when we left the Kampa. Back in Cruzeiro do Sul, I realized I was now on my own, facing the great unknown with no idea how to proceed. Communications with Ailton, so far away, were proving impossible. Poor Macedo was at a loss to know what to do with me or how he could help me; he could only lend a sympathetic ear and try to help me make some sort of plan. My first attempt turned out to be a wild goose chase.

We landed in Tarauacá, a godforsaken little township in the middle of nowhere, an hour's flight from Cruzeiro do Sul. There we were stuck for four days and nights, in searing heat and with nothing to do and no way of getting out. Our arrival had coincided with a political rally. All day and until the small

hours of the morning loudspeakers blared out slogans and tin pan music so loud and jarring it was torture. From the backs of vehicles, attached to poles, on rooftops, the loudspeakers turned up at full volume met us at every street corner; we couldn't get away from them. The town was submerged in noise so shattering it interrupted speech, interfered with sleep and made it impossible even to think straight, and there was no way of getting out or away from it. Every aircraft, regardless of price, was booked by the *politicos*. We were royally stuck, prisoners of this ludicrous situation, with no alternative but to sit it out and stuff earplugs into our ears. Finally it poured with rain and the loudspeakers were mercifully silenced while the dusty streets filled with water and debris. I managed to get some sleep that night for the first time in four days.

We finally managed to procure two seats on a passing aircraft heading back to Cruzeiro do Sul. The last half-mile of the road leading to the airstrip had been washed away by the rain and was impassable. We had to get out of the vehicle that took us there, take off our shoes, roll up our trouser legs and heave our luggage to the airstrip. Time was short and a dark storm was brewing in the sky ahead. I had visions of the aircraft taking off without us. We summoned a group of schoolchildren returning home and asked them to help us. They gallantly loaded up and we trudged together in a straggly line, skidding over the sticky mud that squished between our toes. The aircraft propellors were turning when we arrived on the tarmac. The pilot was nervous and tense at the delay. 'Can't you see the rain ahead? We're late, we've got to get to Cruzeiro before dark,' he yelled at us, shoving us towards the plane with our muddy feet and bags. We took off down a runway inches deep in water as if we were water-skiing.

We flew for an hour through a spectacular rainstorm that kept us on edge throughout the journey. We dived into great banks of ominous black clouds that obliterated all vision for long stretches of time. The rain pounded on the windscreen like hailstones. When we emerged I caught sight of the immense primeval forest stretching below us to the horizon. Visions of a sudden forced descent into this verdant ocean kept appearing in my mind. I stole furtive glances at the young pilot sitting beside me, trying to detect any signs of alarm. He had calmed down and remained cool and unperturbed, keeping the nose of the plane on a steady course westards. He was obviously accustomed to such flying conditions. For the first time in my life I was able to witness the miraculous cycle of rain in the making. Delicate water vapours emanated from the trees and coiled upwards to join the white clouds that slowly darkened and fell again as rain.

I had taken a friend with me from London to help me with the language, but when she fell and broke her arm I had to send her back to Paris. Now I was really on my own. My Portuguese was still poor, but I was beginning to understand quite a lot and managed with considerable effort to make myself understood. Back in Cruzeiro it took me another twenty-four hours to adapt to my new situation. I called Ailton again and informed him of my intention to move into the state of Amazonas, to the north of Acre, to visit the Marubo tribe. I had seen a photograph of a lovely girl with naked breasts and strings of white beads passing through her nose and looped across her face on either ear. Her face was framed in dark hair and she looked out at me with deep, sultry, dark eyes. 'She is my sister,' a young girl working in Macedo's office said to me, 'I am a Marubo myself' (but dressed in western clothes). 'I can take you to her village. I come from there; we can either fly, or walk for six days.'

'Let's try and fly,' I suggested.

I sat in Cruzeiro, camping on the floor of Macedo's office for four weeks with no electricity or water, before I was able to locate an aircraft which would airlift me to the tiny little-known strip hacked out of the jungle on the Curuça river, half an hour's flight north of Cruzeiro. The risk was too great: the pilots all said, 'We don't like flying to unkown strips we are not familiar with, because if we lose the aircraft, who will pay for it?'

'All I need now is an accident,' I thought.

Overleaf Kampa mother and child.

THE KAMPA

The Kampa are one of the great Arawak-speaking nations of the Amazon, whose members were once scattered from Florida and the islands of the Caribbean in the north to the lowlands of Bolivia in the south.

Some archaeologists believe that the centre for the Arawak peoples' dispersal lay in the Amazon floodplain, where the rich alluvial soils established from thousands of years of erosion in the Andes provided a fertile base on which their numbers built up. Powerful migrations of Arawak peoples, it is thought, swept up the major Amazon tributaries, south to the Chaco, north to the watershed of the Orinoco and so down into the Caribbean basin and west to the Amazon's very headwaters. Their progress is marked today by the appliqué pottery found in the sites of their once-populous settlements.

It is here, near the sources of the Amazon, that the Kampa live today. Numbering about 45,000 in all, they inhabit some 12,000 square miles (about 30,000 square kilometres) of mainly upland forests and savannahs in the foothills of the Andes. Most of the Kampa in fact live in Peru, the majority of them in the so-called *ceja de la selva* – 'the eyebrow of the jungle' – where steep Andean streams and rivers sweep down to the lower-lying and hotter Amazonian forests below. Being so close to the Andes, the Kampa have been strongly influenced by the beliefs and ways of their highland Indian neighbours. Most obviously they have adopted the *kushma*, a cotton garment woven on a backstrap loom, which distinguishes them from other Amazonian peoples, most of whom never saw the need for clothing before contact with whites. Kampa is not the name by which these people refer to themselves, but was apparently applied to them by Indian neighbours who thought them 'disshevelled'. In Peru they call themselves 'Ashaninca' and consider the term 'Kampa' to be impolite. In Brazil, however, where some 300 of them live along the Amonia river on the Peruvian border, the name Kampa continues to be used.

An Indian boy among Inca ruins in Pampaconas, Peru, photographed in 1911. Most of the Kampa still live in Peru, where they have been strongly influenced by their highland Indian neighbours.

Despite their complex religious beliefs which show such strong Andean influences, the Kampa's economy, like that of most Amazonian peoples, is based on shifting cultivation with cassava as the staple crop. Cassava is planted from cuttings of the stems thrust into the weak, acidic soils in clumps of two or three together. Except for weeding, the crop demands no further attention until harvest, the starchy tubers becoming large enough to unearth after between ten months and a year. Since the tubers contain cyanide-bearing compounds, the risk of pests is also minimal, although ants and wild pigs take their share, but the crop does demand very careful processing to make it edible. After having their tough, very poisonous and inedible skins peeled off, the tubers must be macerated and pulverized, either by hand on graters or by allowing them to soak first and then mashing them with poles. The mash must then be pressed to squeeze out as much of the cyanide as possible. The juice, which often contains a very fine starch, is only edible if boiled for a very long time to vaporize the poison. The mash, on the other hand, must be sifted to separate out the largest fibres, and the coarse flour which remains must be cooked over a high heat to drive off the remaining cyanide. Toasted in great vessels while stirred with a paddle, the flour yields manioc, which can keep, despite the humidity of the Amazon, for many months. Baked on flat griddles, now made mainly of iron, the flour yields a coarse unleavened cake that is the daily bread over most of Amazonia. Just how a poisonous root which requires complex processing to be edible came to be the staple crop for half a continent remains one of the Amazon's mysteries.

The Kampa first appear in history in 1635, when Franciscan missionaries pushed east of the Andes into the Amazon headwaters in search of further fields for conversion. But after less than ninety years and serious epidemics the Kampa had had enough. They rose up against the Spanish, burning the missions and killing the priests. Rubber provided the next reason for intrusions on to their lands. Not only were the lowland forests of western Amazonia particularly rich in the wild rubber trees, but the valleys inhabited by the Kampa provided a natural export route across the high Andes and down to the Pacific. Thus, while many of the lower-living Kampa were subjected to the exploitation and violence associated with rubber extraction, those in the hills fought a one-sided battle against the Peruvian armed forces to prevent the takeover of their lands. Since that time the Kampa have been obliged to share their lands with the whites. The violence escalated for a short but terrible period at the end of the rubber boom, in about 1912, when the price of rubber fell dramatically as the market was flooded with rubber grown on plantations in the Far East. Slaving intensified, causing terrible suffering to those subjected to the raids. As one chronicler recorded:

> To realise these slave-drives, the rubber gatherers use big canoes . . . full of savages, all well-armed with modern shotguns and with big supplies for the expedition, and under the orders of some chief already half-civilized, in other words corrupt and bad, without a soul and destitute of any humanitarian feeling . . . . when night extends its dark and tenebrous coat and when the poor savages are given to their sweet dreams ignorant of their fate, the [raiders] approach, encircling from all sides the hut or huts, and at a signal fall on their poor victims full of fright and horror and cut the breathing in their throats and the blood in the veins. The terrifying picture that develops in the middle of obscurity and confusion is impossible for the pen to describe. Cries of indignation, expressed as if by wild animals, pleadings, lamentations, tears. Once this terrifying massacre is finished, the assailants take the children and women by force, they rape the latter, tie them up like beasts and lead them precipitously to the canoes while hitting them all the while. And then they sell these poor human captives as if they were animals.

The 300 Kampa of Brazil are one isolated group who survived this period of desolation. Their lands were finally demarcated by the Brazilian government's Indian agency in 1985. During the 1960s and 1970s, the Kampa maintained their links with the Brazilian economy by selling mahogany and cedar from their forests to timber merchants in the local towns and wage labouring in Cruzeiro do Sul. However, with the help of pro-Indian activists, they are now engaged in a successful enterprise to revive their communities' economies by selling other forest products to the regional centres. Despite centuries of exploitation and interference the Kampa have held on to their religion, identity, customs and pride.

Left A Kampa girl.

Preceding pages A Kampa mother and child. The 300 or so Kampa who live in Brazil have managed to survive a long and troubled history of persecution and exploitation. The tribe's first contact with westerners came in the seventeenth century, when Spanish missionaries pushed east of the Andes into the Amazon headwaters in search of souls. Within a century the Indians had had enough of them and the devastating epidemics of disease they brought with them, and rose up against them. Then came the rubber boom, when rubber barons, greedy for this natural wealth that occurred with such abundance on Kampa territory, invaded their lands with the aid of the Peruvian armed forces. Many Kampa were killed, and many more were taken into slavery in order to service the needs of the industry. Slave raids continued well into this century.

Overleaf Probably no one knows the exact age of this old woman, as the Indians do not keep a tally of their age. Old people are assured a place in the community and are not expected to take part in the more strenuous chores, though grandmothers help their daughters and daughters-in-law out with domestic tasks and take care of their grandchildren.

Preceding pages, opposite and above Sometimes Indian parents are reluctant to allow their babies to be photographed, as they feel it may jeopardize their spirits. The link between young children's spirits and their bodies is believed to be still very weak, and there is the constant danger that a child's spirit may be lured away by a forest being, leaving the child to sicken and die. To guard against this the parents have to observe strict taboos concerning diet and sex. As children grow older their spirits become more secure in their bodies, but they are not thought to be spiritually independent until they reach the age of three. Until then they accompany their parents or grandparents as they go about their daily tasks, often held close to their bodies in slings.

The Kampa's strongly chiselled features, emphasized by their natural solemnity, bear witness to their Peruvian ancestry. Despite centuries of exploitation and interference they have retained their pride, along with their religion, customs and identity.

Above and opposite Rafael was never without his pipe.

The Amazon and its tributaries remain the main routes for travel and communication for the forest peoples, and dugout canoes remain the principal mode of transport. Learning how to make a canoe, and how to handle it with the skill and dexterity needed to negotiate fast-flowing currents and hazardous rapids, is an important part of every boy's education.

Above, opposite and overleaf While many of the forest peoples of Amazonia paint their entire bodies with complex designs, the Kampa, who clothe their bodies with *kushmas*, concentrate on their faces. They obtain the intensely red pigment they habitually use from the fruits of the *anatto* plant, which they cultivate for the purpose.

Above and opposite Parrots are often kept as pets. They are also sometimes hunted for food, though they are inedible unless cooked for hours. The Indians never eat animals that they have raised as part of their families, however, as in their view this would be akin to cannibalism. It is for this reason that, although they have tame animals, they never keep domestic animals for food.

Overleaf Both men and women are skilled in many crafts, using raw materials from the forest or their cultivated gardens; wood to make everything from canoes to blowpipes, cotton to make slings and clothes, and cane and lianas to make baskets, sieves and manioc presses.

Above and opposite The Kampa grow the cotton for their
kushmas in the gardens they clear in the forest, patiently spinning it
on to a wooden spindle before weaving it into rough cloth.

Preceding pages The brilliantly coloured feathers of forest birds
such as macaws, deftly strung and knotted to make garlands,
headdresses and armbands, bear witness to the prowess of young
hunters and are much-coveted trophies.

Above and opposite The Kampa are especially skilled at
spinning and weaving cotton, which they dye in characteristically
grave colours with vegetable pigments extracted from forest plants.

Preceding pages Kampa homes are simple and uncluttered,
containing only the bare essentials of life. The hammocks are
sometimes draped with gauze for protection against mosquitoes
and other flying insects.

Above and opposite From the age of three children spend most of their time together, playing in the village and exploring the forest or riverbank. This creates a valuable bond between them, as well as encouraging the social skills and sense of sharing and mutual dependence that are essential for communal living.

Preceding pages Giorgio the *pagé*, or shaman, lived on his compound with his mother, who cared for him and his brother's children. Shamans are the Indians' spiritual specialists, who know how to control the forces of nature and restore health to the sick. They can move at will through the spirit world to combat the vengeful animal spirits that cause illness, gaining access to this world through the use of powerful hallucinogenic drugs.

Overleaf Giorgio sharing his simple meal with his nephew. The Indians' diet depends heavily on cassava in various forms. The starchy tubers contain cyanide-bearing compounds and need lengthy and complex processing to be made edible. Quite how this poisonous root became the staple crop for half a continent remains one of the Amazon's mysteries.

One of cassava's many uses is to make a potent fermented drink, with saliva as the fermenting agent. Once shredded, boiled and pulped, the cassava is thoroughly chewed and spat out. The resulting mush is then left to ferment in the sun.

Familiarity with the traditional longbows and arrows starts from an early age. The Indians are superlative hunters, with an intimate and comprehensive understanding of the forest and the animals that inhabit it. They tip their arrows with poisons derived from forest plants which disable their prey but do not taint the meat, as they are harmless when taken into the system by mouth.

Overleaf Small boys use catapults to shoot unsuspecting birds from the trees. Hunting is a passion from an early age.

This mother kept flicking her scarf over her sleeping child to ward off the *carapana* flies which constantly attack exposed skin. Swarms of biting insects are one of the more irritating aspects of the teeming life of the forest.

Preceding pages A Kampa family group.

There was an immense tenderness in the
relationship between Giorgio's old mother
and her grandson.

Overleaf Three stages in the production of
the fermented drink the Kampa make from
cassava tubers.

Preceding pages, above and opposite
Giorgio preparing the hallucinogenic
ayahuasca infusion from leaves and bark
gathered in the forest. Such drugs give
shamans access to the spirit world, where
they can do battle with the vengeful spirits
that cause illness and gain control over
other natural forces. Forest peoples, and
especially their shamans, can identify huge
numbers of plants with useful or medicinal
purposes, some of which have already been
adopted by western medicine for the
treatment of malaria, infantile leukaemia
and many other conditions. Threats to the
rainforest and to traditional Indian
communities also put at risk both this
immense body of knowledge and the plants
themselves.

Overleaf far right Giorgio applied his
make-up everyday.

Preceding pages, left and above The rivers of the Amazon basin are the arteries of the rainforest. The Amazon and its tributaries, several of which are navigable for over 3000 miles (5000 kilometres) of their length, carry one-fifth of all the earth's running water. To the Indians they are both an essential source of water and food and the best means of travel and communication.

Overleaf A Kampa boy in the forest.

Pages 102-3 Gardens are cleared with axes in old-growth forest and planted with food crops which require only small amounts of nutrients: yams, sweet potatoes, bananas, plantains, cocoyams and the ever-present cassava.

Pages 104-5 Tenderness towards babies and between brothers and sisters or friends is very evident among the Indians.

Flight into the unknown

Linda Mar, just fifteen years old, was the daughter of the Marubo village leader on the Curuça river. Bright and self-assured, she confirmed without hesitation the existence of an airstrip and laughingly shrugged off the pilot's misgivings. Who was I to listen to? After much hesitation, I opted for Linda Mar's version and we finally convinced a pilot from Rio Branco, two hours' flight from Cruzeiro, to come and pick us up. He listened intently to Linda Mar but with reservations. There was no sign of any airstrip on his aerial map. He finally agreed to attempt the sortie and we set off towards the unknown. I had sat in Cruzeiro do Sul for weeks and weeks since my return from the Kampa and was desperate to get out. In moments like these, one throws caution to the wind and becomes unusually daring.

The flight, we calculated, should not take more than thirty minutes and ninety minutes later, when, flying low over the endless green canopy we had still not sighted any sign of human habitation, let alone an airstrip, I began to get worried. Fears of another abortive trip started creeping into me. 'Let's turn back and follow the river south towards Cruzeiro,' I meekly suggested to the pilot, 'We may have overshot it.' The aircraft veered round and we scanned the scene below us in silence. In the back Linda Mar remained calm and confident that we would eventually sight the airstrip.

Sure enough, just as she had said, suddenly a clearing appeared along the river banks, like a hole in the vast green canvas. A large thatched *maloca* stood in the centre with smaller constructions around it. We could pick out the people in the beaten earth compound and canoes on the water and then the airstrip, a rectangular cleft about 250 yards long. A sigh of relief and down we dropped, the pilot positioning the aircraft for maximum clearance of the runway. The tops of the trees rushed up at us and we touched down to a bumpy landing, charging through the long grass that swept the belly of the plane and coming to a halt with only a few yards to spare at the end of the strip.

The Marubo villagers appeared from among the trees and ventured hesitantly on to the strip. Recognizing Linda Mar they clustered around us and helped us unload our bags. I asked the pilot to return for us in a week. We had no other means of contacting him. He flew off and left me there with the Indians in the middle of the Amazonian rainforest. It was a strange sensation, but I had no qualms about it. We watched him taxi down the whole length of the short runway and lift off, barely clearing the trees as he climbed back into the sky.

I followed my new companions through the forest on a winding path padded with centuries of decaying leaves. It was an epic walk into the core of the jungle, hemmed in on all sides by the trees and thick green leaves. I was moving towards that rarefied world of my imagination where the ugly trappings of my civilization had not yet arrived. I felt suddenly satisfied. Being so totally cut off enhanced that feeling and eliminated all fear and apprehension. I was now in the hands of the Indians, these gentle naked people of the forest, with their almond eyes and strings of white beads passing through their noses, who were carrying my bags and camera cases on their heads, leading me to their homes, not questioning my unannounced visit or motives. How vulnerable they were, in their acceptance of my presence, I thought. I felt not only fortunate but privileged to be among them, and couldn't help thinking how the photographs I was going to take back with me were going to expose them to my world, and therefore inevitably contaminate them with the pressures of my culture.

The heat and humidity were devastating and the insects infernal. I was getting my first real taste of jungle living. Everything before now had seemed like a walk in Hyde Park. I had stepped into an insane, abrasive, insect-swatting waltz which quickly brought back the itching pink welts that were to give me no respite for the duration of my stay. But as the villagers clustered around me I knew I had come to the right place.

As with the Kampa, the atmosphere was gentle and congenial. I felt quickly accepted and was able to get on with my work without inhibition. The group was not large: it was the end of the dry season and many of them had moved to more fertile fishing grounds further upstream. I was able to focus in on those elements that had first caught my eye, and when I later looked at my pictures I knew why I had gone there.

Their daily life did not differ much from that of the Kampa, consisting mainly of simple domestic chores that kept them busy from morning to evening. They tended to their manioc plants which they grew in clearings in the forest, collecting the roots, which they boiled like sweet potatoes into an ivory-coloured mush in great black pots on open wood fires; the juice is highly toxic, so the roots are grated to a pulp and squeezed through a wooden press to extract the poisonous liquid. The mash is then thoroughly dried in large cast-iron trays over a roaring fire, much as one would roast coffee beans, to remove the last of the poison. The results is manioc flour. Mixed with water this makes a smooth white dough which is rolled out into flat pancakes and roasted over an open fire on flat trays, like pitta bread. Huge bunches of cooking bananas are also brought in on the backs of the women and turned into a fermented drink.

Endless time is spent fashioning their characteristic minute white beads from riverine snail shells. These are crushed into tiny pieces and pierced with a sharp metallic point attached to the end of a stick that is rubbed between the open palms of the hands. They are then strung together on a thread and rubbed down with pumice stone until they are perfectly rounded.

Three times a day at least, visits are paid to the river, where pots and pans are scrubbed with river sand until they shine. The same goes for the strings of beads which they uncoil from behind their ears and allow to hang into the water from their noses while they scrub them shiny white with the sand. Then they wash themselves, splashing around with obvious relish. Finally, when the river has settled and cleared, they fill their earthenware jars with water and carry them home on one shoulder, keeping them steady with one hand and pressed against the side of the head.

The men go hunting with their dogs approximately twice a week and come back with monkeys, birds and wild boar. The return of the hunters, sometimes after nightfall, is always heralded by a lot of fuss, as if to show appreciation for the effort entailed in feeding the community. The dogs are themselves keen hunters and quiver with excitement and anticipation at the onset of each day's hunt, returning limp and panting, exhausted by the day's exertion.

Observing these daily activities took my mind off my own discomforts and helped me to ignore them. Meals were always taken inside the main hut. The women sit in a circle apart from the men, around a bowl of stew and a type of 'polenta' made from the manioc powder. Fish caught in the river is roasted whole, scales and intestines included, over open fires, as is the meat. Both are sometimes wrapped in banana leaves and placed over the flames until the leaves began to disintegrate. When the day's hunt is good, what is not eaten is slowly smoked and dried for consumption on leaner days. As with the Kampa there was a wonderful sense of calm and togetherness, and I never noticed any tension or dissent between them, either among the men or the women, together or apart.

Linda Mar's presence greatly helped the rapport between us and I soon felt part of the family. I gave them little gifts from my store of provisions and coloured glass beads I had brought from England. In exchange they brought me gifts of fruit and their own white beads; necklaces, arm bands and anklets were shyly produced and knotted around my wrists and neck. The exchange was especially meaningful because it was so completely unsolicited. I felt they really wanted me to have something of theirs to remember them by. These were gifts from the heart. These tiny beads that had taken them so painstakingly long to make from riverine shells, and which they had then strung on to homespun threads from home-grown cotton, held so much more value for me than anything simply bought in a shop that I could give them. It was a moving and generous gesture that I shall always remember. How long, I wondered, would it be before this traditional way of life vanished? Linda Mar, who had discarded her urban mini skirt, her lipstick, her shoes and T-shirt on arrival, pranced around among her people bare-breasted and barefoot and covered in white beads. She seemed to symbolize the changes that would inevitably follow as the trappings of western culture encroached on theirs through missionaries and government institutions aiming to 'domesticate' them in order to have better control over them.

The distant drone of an approaching aircraft brought everyone scurrying out into the open, their faces turned skywards. It was time to say goodbye, gather up my belongings and head for the airstrip. I was secretly relieved; my arms and legs were swollen from insect bites, and the heat and humidity intensified by the previous night's heavy rainfall was making me tense and edgy. All my years in Africa had not prepared me for such extreme climatic conditions. Here in the Amazon forest the rain fell like a waterfall and the heat and humidity it generated were so thick they were almost tangible and impossible to ignore.

As the aircraft left the ground and climbed over the now familiar trees into the rain clouds above, I looked down one last time at my new friends standing with upturned faces etched with strings of tiny white beads, and felt satisfied and pleased.

Overleaf Arriana was the prettiest girl I met on my whole African journey.

THE MARUBO

The valley of the Javari river, which flows north along the Brazilian border with Peru to join the Amazon at the town of Benjamin Constant, remains one of the most remote and unfrequented areas of the Amazon basin. Isolated groups of Indians, who spurn contact with the outside world, still live in the dense lowland forests along the banks of the narrow winding rivers that cross the region. Some of these groups remain completely uncontacted, and thus unidentified, by outsiders.

The Marubo, who today number only some 600 people, live on the southern edge of this region, spread out in twenty small communities in the upper courses of rivers which drain north down to the Javari and the Amazon. Traditionally they live in large, cone-shaped communal dwellings, usually set near the summit of one of the many low hills that undulate across the area.

Like most Amazonian groups, the Marubo do not have chiefs vested with much authority over others, but the communities do coalesce around the personality of leaders who strengthen their positions by securing loyalties through ties of marriage and trade. It is a complex social system that they have to manipulate to achieve this elusive power.

The Marubo all trace their origins back to nine mythological heroes, each of whom gave his name to the clans of descendants who came after him. Marriages are arranged only between different clans, which in turn are each divided into two parts. For according to the Marubo system, parents and children are defined in different sections of society, a woman's children being in the same section as her parents, just as she is in the same section as her grandchildren. A Marubo child thus grows up with a strong sense of belonging in the society, his identity being not only in the hearth group of his immediate parents, but also in his clan and section.

During collective rituals, the Marubo recount lengthy myths which recall the past, establishing the ancestry of the clans and their separate identities. The myths are sung out, line by line, by an older member of the community and repeated in chorus by all the others gathered there. As among the Yanomami Indians, a major occasion for these gatherings of neighbouring villages is to consume the ground-up ashes of the bones of previously cremated dead relatives. The Marubo are also well known for their shamans and for their complex medicinal lore, which involves the use of a very wide variety of forest plants, herbs, resins, barks and roots.

Although the Marubo do not appear identifiably in the historical records until the turn of this century, it is unlikely that they avoided all contact with white civilization until then. Jesuit missions, sent downriver from the headwaters of the Amazon by the Spanish in Peru, were established near to the Javari valley in the mid-seventeenth century, while Carmelite missions, associated with slave raids, penetrated upriver from the mouth of the Amazon shortly after, partly with the aim of securing as much as possible of the Amazon basin for the Portuguese crown.

It seems probable that the Marubo were once among a number of people who were lumped together variously as Mayoruna or Maxoruna by explorers of the

Pages 112-13 Early morning mist shrouds the village after a heavy night's rain. The Marubo traditionally live in large, cone-shaped communal dwellings.

Pages 114-115 Wooden houses raised on stilts protect their inhabitants from unwelcome visitors such as snakes, spiders, burrowing fleas and biting flies.

period. Yet, once the search for slaves abated, there was little to attract whites into the area. Occasional expeditions to collect sarsaparilla, Brazil nuts and other exotic forest products limited contacts between the Indians and outsiders to the more accessible reaches of the lower rivers. Groups like the Marubo, isolated in the headwaters above the rapids, were apparently little affected.

However, the rubber boom of the late nineteenth century brought the area firmly into the Brazilian economy, and the profit to be gained from the precious latex overcame such physical obstacles. Rubber barons operating off the Amazon established a network of trails, workshops and trading posts all across the Amazon headwaters, and the Javari area was not excluded. All the Indian communities of the area suffered severely during this period. Many Marubo became directly involved in the rubber trade, locked into debt by the traders. The trade had the effect of breaking up the traditional communities. Every family lived alone to collect each day the latex bled from the trees. Economic ties between the Indian tappers and the traders, to whom they lived in debt, took precedence over the social and religious ties of the traditional community. Yet as the rubber economy declined these binding obligations weakened, until by 1938 contact was finally broken off when the trade collapsed.

Indians on the Rio Javari, an illustration from the French explorer Francis de Castelnau's account of his expedition to South America in 1852. The Javari river valley remains one of the most remote and unfrequented areas of the Amazon basin.

The depredations of the rubber era had reduced the Marubo to near extinction, but under an inspiring leader, whose memory is today revered by the Marubo, the Indians reorganized. They re-established themselves in several large settlements and their numbers began to rise again. By the early 1960s there were some 300 individuals and since then their numbers have increased rapidly, reaching 400 by the mid-1970s and rising to just over 600 today.

Sustained contact with the world of the whites was re-established by fundamentalist missionaries in the early 1960s, who now maintain a mission among the Marubo serviced by air from Eirunepe, on the Jurua river to the south. In the early 1970s the whole Marubo area was temporarily overrun by oil prospectors from the Brazilian state oil company and in the mid-1970s, as part of a programme to 'integrate' and 'develop' Amazonia, plans were laid to concentrate and resettle the Marubo, along with other Indian groups from the region, into a small area. The programme, which luckily lapsed before being effectively applied, was justified 'in order to resolve the land problem', the aim being to move the Indians off the greater part of their territory before granting them land rights.

The future of the Marubo, along with other groups of the Javari, depends above all on whether they gain security on their lands. Since the early 1980s it has been proposed that these lands, with those of the numerous other Indian groups of the Javari valley, should be encompassed in a single 'Indian Park'. However, successive moves to establish this area in law by genuinely concerned local officials of the government Indian agency, urged on by church and pro-Indian activists, have been frustrated at higher levels of government. The main problems that the Indians now face in gaining security on their lands are strategic. Oil and gas finds, on the Urucu river east of the area in Brazil and west of the area in Peru, have rekindled industry's hopes of finding oil in the area. At the same time the government still has plans to build a major highway from the Amazon river south into Acre, pushing right through the area of the proposed 'Indian Park'.

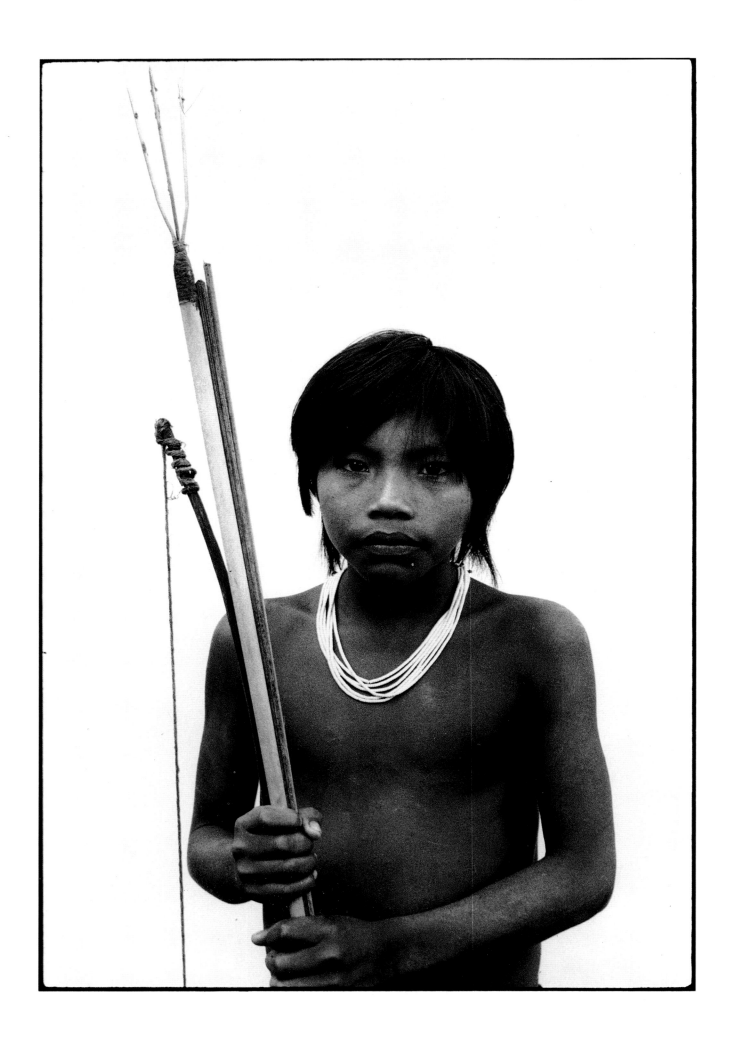

Above and opposite A young Marubo hunter and his father. Hunting is an essential skill for young men, for the Indians are aware that the food crops they cultivate are low in nutrients and must be supplemented by high-protein meat and fish.

Pages 116-23 Daily life among the Indians proceeds at an unhurried pace. The women's time is occupied with domestic chores – cooking, tending the fire, cultivating the garden, weaving and making simple utensils – with plenty of time for playing with the children, chatting and mutual grooming.

Pages 124-5 The elegant pots used for gathering water are made by the women, using clay tempered with burned tree-bark ash. They build the walls of the vessels by coiling the clay round and thinning it with the pressure of their hands and a piece of gourd. When the pots have been fired they are smoked to give them their black glaze.

Above and opposite Loisina, Linda Mar's sister, her three
brothers, Jesus, Antonio and Petronio, and her husband Petrus,
who is dressed for the hunt. Prowess at hunting greatly increases a
young man's eligibility in the eyes of the girls of the village – an
important consideration in a society where men outnumber women
and may also have more than one wife.

Overleaf The complex social structure of the Marubo gives all the children a strong sense of belonging to both their immediate family and a larger clan.

Above and opposite Dogs are a recent introduction, valued for their keen hunting ability in the forest. Among some Indian groups dogs are accorded the same cremation ceremony as humans when they die, and especially good hunters are also honoured with a ceremonial funerary meal.

Overleaf The Marubo paint their faces with an inky liquid made from crushed charcoal. The elaborate patterns and motifs became particularly flamboyant for special occasions, and there are conventions to be observed for specific rituals and ceremonies such as funerals.

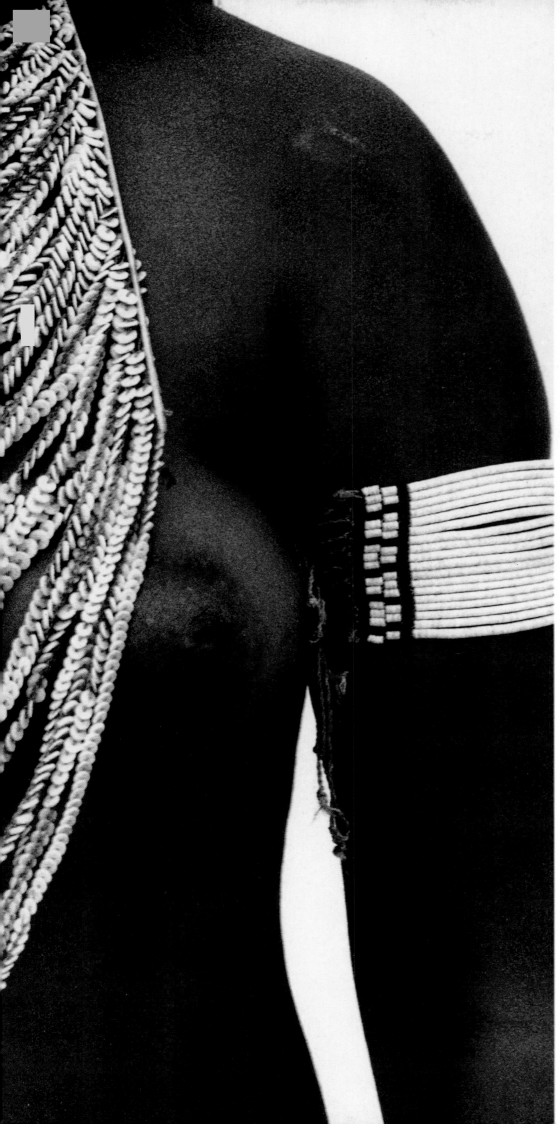

Above, left and overleaf The Marubo spend endless time and exercise considerable skill in fashioning their distinctive tiny white beads. First they collect snail shells from the river and crush them into tiny pieces. Then they pierce them with a sharp metallic point attached to the end of a stick that is rubbed between the open palms of the hands. Finally (overleaf), they string them together on a thread and rub them against a log with a pumice-like stone until they are perfectly rounded.

Loisina painting Petrus.

Preceding pages Decked with beads and with their faces painted, these three little girls were irresistible. They fixed the camera with an intense, unwavering gaze as if they expected something to pop out at them.

Overleaf The Indians get a lot of fun out of life. They laugh a lot and are seldom

A little Marubo girl. The Marubo have survived invasions by rubber tappers and oil prospectors and their numbers are now increasing. Their future depends above all on whether they can succeed in securing their rights to their lands, now threatened by government plans to build a major highway through them, and by oil and gas finds near by, which have rekindled industry's hopes of finding oil in the area.

Preceding pages The luxuriant canopy of the rainforest protects seedlings, ferns and fungi from the hot sun. Plants thrive in the hothouse atmosphere created by the tropical sun and heavy rainfall: a patch of rainforest some 4 miles or 6.5 kilometres square may contain as many as 1500 different species of flowering plant and over 750 species of tree. All these species, together with the animals and insects that inhabit them, feed on them, pollinate them and spread their seeds, are bound together in a complex and delicately balanced web of interdependence. It is this balance, understood and respected by the indians over many centuries, that is now threatened by western interference.

Inside the *maloca*

We dropped Linda Mar at Cruzeiro do Sul. I picked up the rest of my belongings from the rubber tappers' headquarters and flew on to Rio Branco with my pilot. Having tried in vain to contact Ailton to give him a progress report, I flew on to Pôrto Vehlo where I checked into a charming little hotel. I was now in the state of Rondônia, where I thought I might try and investigate the Surúi and Uru-eu-wau-wau tribes, but soon discovered that unless I had a more positive lead to them it would be difficult, if not impossible, to penetrate the barrier of western indoctrination that had already affected them and outwardly transformed them into shorted and shirted members of my own western culture. My peripheral enquiries were met with meaningful resistance, and I found myself up against the eternal complexes that always arise from white interference in other cultures. 'Why', they all wanted to know, 'was I so interested in the archaic aspect of their culture when the contemporary one was so much more representative of them today?' No manner of explanation could convince them. I was about to give up my quest when an unexpected phone call arrived in an office I happened to be in. A friendly, encouraging English voice jerked at my sagging morale, and I left town that same night by bus for Pimenta Bueno, 700 kilometres south.

Nick Burch was at the crowded bus stop of the frontier town at six o'clock in the morning to pick me up in his clapped-out Landcruiser. Barefoot and tousled, wearing a pair of crumpled white slacks and no shirt, he looked as if he had just rolled out of bed, but his greeting was warm and welcoming and interested. I felt an immediate sympathy with him. Nick was one of those eccentric adventurers who are the spiritual descendants of the empire-builders once responsible for Britain's eminence abroad. His name had been given to me by a friend in London as a possible interesting contact, for over the past twenty years he had single-handedly been struggling with a reforestation project that he had himself originated in an effort to do something tangible to combat the destruction of the Brazilian rainforest. He had already replenished his area with over a million mahogany trees and had another million seedlings in his nursery waiting to be transplanted. Nick was a visionary, who like so many of his ilk suffered from a perennial lack of funds that clipped his wings and prevented him from soaring to the heights that his far-sighted concepts deserved.

I spent a fascinating week with him and learned a lot about the rainforest dilemma, but my contact with the Surúi Indians in the region only intensified my feeling that what I was looking for had long since vanished: I realized to my dismay that I was five or ten years too late. I moved on, refreshed but still confused, and determined not to let the obstacles I was facing deter me. I headed north to Roraima, the northernmost state of Brazil on the Venezuelan border, where in Boa Vista I prepared to visit the much-publicized Yanomami tribe, today one of the largest remaining tribes of the Amazon, under siege from white infiltration that is slowly poisoning them and threatening their existence.

Here in Boa Vista I had previously arranged to meet with Davi Yanomami, their spokesman whom I had first met with Ailton in London. I had planned my visit to coincide with his return from a rainforest symposium in Paris. He was my only link with the tribe and I had to rely entirely on him to show me the way and open the doors. I was therefore rather taken aback by a certain coolness in his manner when I appeared, which considerably unnerved me. I had been warned that I would need all the tact and diplomacy at my disposal in approaching the Yanomami, so I moved forward with caution and much hesitation. Having suffered so much because of white encroachment they were suspicious of people like me; I was aware that I was treading on delicate and much-abused terrain.

Roraima was one of the most undeveloped states of Brazil until ten or fifteen years ago when the *garimpeiros* (gold miners) discovered and began to unearth its vast mineral wealth. It spiralled into the headlines when staggering amounts of gold began leaving its boundaries each week. The *garimpeiros*, many of whom had lived in abject poverty, became millionaires overnight, and inevitably violence and greed began to take their toll.

People from all over Brazil flocked in hordes to the diminutive dusty frontier settlement, and Boa Vista exploded into a boom town. Hastily erected concrete buildings and shacks mushroomed around wide tarred boulevards without any rationale other than the glint of gold.

Then the government changed and cracked down on the *garimpeiros*, whose giddy rise to wealth and prosperity had unleashed an unrestrained lust for power and possessions. Individual mining was outlawed, ostensibly because it was interfering with and destroying the Yanomami tribes living in the forests they were pillaging. I later learned from the incensed *garimpeiros* that this was only a government ploy to remove them from the area in order to hand it over to its accomplices, the multinational conglomerates eager to move in with heavy machinery. Many successful *garimpeiros* consequently moved elsewhere, taking their new-found wealth with them, and within a year Boa Vista ground to a virtual halt. What remained of the once-bustling boom town, which used to be so overcrowded that at night the streets were everywhere slung with hammocks, bore out the tales of woe that reached my ears.

With the help of Claudia Andujar, a naturalized Hungarian-Brazilian photographer whom I met in Boa Vista, and who for thirty years has been working with the Yanomami and was a friend of Davi's, I was able to make a plan. I hoped to visit the Demini Yanomami *maloca*, where Claudia was helping Davi to implement a medical assistance programme that he had originated. Claudia seemed diffident and slightly aloof at first, but she knew my book on Africa and was curious to know more about my project. Her photographic coverage of the Yanomami had earned her quite a reputation in Brazil, but I was not familiar with her work apart from a beautiful poster I had once seen in São Paulo, which resembled my own style, I thought. She was a great help in bridging the gap between Davi and myself.

It nevertheless took me another week before I was able to leave again for the daunting confines of the rainforest. These interludes in towns always made me feel nervous and full of misgivings. Each time it was all so new and unfamiliar. But as usual luck was on my side. This time I met an Indian nurse working for FUNAI, the government agency that 'pacified' and 'integrated' the Indians and hypothetically saw to their welfare, and WHO SPOKE ENGLISH. Here name was Dekka and she had been working in Demini for the past four years. Dekka had a close relationship with the Yanomami of the area, whom she considered as her extended family. She travelled with me on the plane I had hired to fly me to their *maloca*. We immediately struck up a friendship that proved invaluable to me, and on which I depended utterly to help me breach the delicate barrier that separated our two worlds. She was a godsend.

After an hour-and-a-half flight over the green canopy, the aircraft dropped us at the little FUNAI outpost, set in the middle of the jungle against a spectacular mountain of grey-blue stone. We taxied to a halt in front of three tin-roofed wooden houses where Dekka and her two Indian assistants lived, and then watched the plane fly off again, leaving us together in the long grass with our bags around us. A heavy stillness permeated the air and the slightest sounds of insects were audible. It was a weird and exhilarating feeling, and the now familiar sensation that I had once again come to the right place made my heart sing, despite the crushing heat.

I set off eagerly behind Dekka *en route* for the *maloca*, a forty-minute march from the FUNAI post. She led me on another epic walk through the forest, accompanying it with a fascinating commentary on the many and varied facets of jungle living. She pointed out the different trees and leaves and vines used by the Yanomami, punctuating her comments with little personal anecdotes. The magnificent trees towering above us cut out the hot midday sun and allowed us to walk in the cool, mottled shade of their leaves. We followed a little path, stepping over fallen logs and stopping to rest on the buttresses of the giant trees that fanned upwards from the damp pungent soil, like the solid wings of some prehistoric bird whose neck stretched a hundred feet into the sky. We listened to the call of the invisible parrots and watched brilliantly coloured butterflies settle on delicate mushrooms and mosses.

Suddenly a family of Indians appeared from among the trees, walking silently towards us. A child of about five years of age walked in front, carrying a younger one on its back. The mother followed with a large woven basket piled high with firewood, on top of which a smaller child was tucked between the logs. Their lithe, ochre-coloured bodies were completely naked, except for a little fringe a few inches long tied with a string around their skinny hips, leaving their buttocks bare.

They stopped and chatted with Dekka and then quietly moved on. It was an encouraging introduction, and when we later came across Genesio, ten feet up a monumental tree at which he was hacking, I knew I was on the right path. He jumped to the ground and climbed towards us over the branches and bushes he had felled in an effort to clear the land for more edible plants. Genesio too was completely naked, except for a string attached to the end of his penis and tied around his hips, with a wad of tobacco leaves tucked into his bottom lip. He was gentle and friendly and showed us the way to a crystal-clear spring flowing through the undergrowth. The heat had hit its daily high; we took off our clothes and lay down in the cool, transparent water and quenched our burning thirst. It was such a natural thing to do in this pristine setting and it instantly set the pattern for what lay ahead. Our path threaded through banana and manioc plantations between the trees before we finally reached the great *maloca*.

The *maloca* was another astonishing revelation. Small, wiry white and tan dogs ran out and barked at us, baring vicious fangs as we appeared from among the huge banana leaves. In a clearing beside the stream the thatched roof rose like a huge leafy dome. We entered it through one of the small doors in the side. Nothing on the outside had prepared me for what met my eyes: as I advanced into this vast amphitheatre in the jungle I experienced the same sensation that I had had when I first stepped into St Peter's in Rome. A feeling of awed reverence brought me to a halt and left me speechless. The great circular thatched construction, supported by long straight poles, soared upwards around me for what must have been about one hundred feet. The centre was open to the sky and the Yanomami lived together round small hearths in the shade of the great sloping roof, their hammocks strung between the rafters and poles. It was an astonishing and ingenious example of jungle architecture.

I immediately felt uneasy, intruding among them with my cameras and my western façade: I seemed so out of place in this solemn setting where the inhabitants blended so harmoniously with their surrounds. They were all naked, their skins rubbed with an amber-copper glow that radiated from the shadows and spilled into the bright, sunlit central circle, appearing like shadows in an ancient dream until my eyes adjusted to the change of light. It was an extraordinary sight that commanded respect and momentarily unnerved me. There were to be many such sensations over the next two weeks. This was indeed the world of my fantasies; each new tribe I visited confirmed and justified my determination to carry on trying to capture this way of life with my camera before it is inevitably changed for ever, in the face of obstacles that sometimes seemed unsurmountable. *Fortuna audaces invat* (fortune helps the daring).

I did not, however, yet know how much the difficult daily living conditions I was going to have to deal with would affect my efforts, and looking back at my adventure I am conscious now of the extent to which I was stretching myself. The physical strain was enormous, and I often felt both discouraged and debilitated, and longed for it all to be over.

Letting the emotional surge of my initial reaction settle before I picked up my cameras, I just walked around, taking it all in and allowing the Yanomami to get a good look at me, greeting them with smiles and the odd Brazilian word. Trying to take a discreet interest in their activities without seeming intrusive, I met their initial reserve by remaining close to Dekka who acted as a sort of chaperone. It felt much like being a new girl at school again, and I knew time would ease the tension. For a while it seemed best to spend the nights with Dekka at the little FUNAI post and walk the three miles to and fro through the forest each day. I managed to keep this up for a week, when the physical strain finally got to me and I decided to ask if I could move to the *maloca*.

Dekka spoke to the head of the *maloca*, Lori Var, and asked him if he could see any inconvenience in my move. He consented softly and next day, with the help of Genesio, I moved my belongings, tent, cameras, bedding and food by wheelbarrow on a comical jaunt through the forest. My sense of humour got the better of me as I tried to picture myself marching behind the naked Genesio as he pushed his squeaking wheelbarrow before him, and together we had a good laugh over the ludicrous situation.

We came upon a group of children playing with a large fallen palm frond beside a small lake. They were pulling it behind them like a cart, giving each other rides and squeaking with laughter that resembled the calls of the hidden birds in the trees. All around them giant palms and bushes with large fan-shaped leaves rose from the water's edge. We stopped and watched them for a while until they noticed us and scuttled back into the protective embrace of the forest. It was a magical interlude drawn from the beginnings of time, an image that will remain embedded in my memory and will take me into my old age. 'We are all responsible for the vitality we create in our lives,' one of my collaborators commented as he looked at the pictures of this scene.

Once in the *maloca*, I pitched my little dome tent among the Yanomami hammocks. I would have preferred to keep a certain distance in order to avoid intruding too obviously on them and to retain a modicum of privacy, but there was no place suitable outside, and I had no alternative. Pitching the tent and unpacking proved fascinating to the Indians, and they circled around me, shyly offering to help. We laid a bed of banana leaves beneath the tent, and as we unfolded it I was glad to see that the medley of jungle leaves and flowers I had painted on the garish yellow nylon covering in São Paulo fitted nicely into the scenery. The inflatable mattress and the footpump were a source of much merriment, and the Yanomami could not understand why I did not sleep in a hammock like them, as I could not sleep in the curved position. This little charade accompanied by hoots of laugher did a lot to establish the camaraderie so essential to my work. With unrestrained curiosity they fingered everything, trying on my hats, brushing their hair with my brush, peering into the little mirror, sniffing at the face cream. They hated the smell of my citronella oil and refused to let me touch them when I was wearing it; this blessed repellent that saved my sanity was also, to my alarm, repelling them.

I spent ten days in the *maloca*, difficult uncomfortable days that sapped my energy and often made me edgy and tense, but which allowed me to observe the daily life of the Indians at close quarters. Devoured by the ruthless insects despite my citronella oil, hot and dirty and badly fed on the minimal meals I prepared for myself of rice, spaghetti, potatoes and bananas, I felt exhausted but managed to keep smiling.

Fortunately I had the muesli bars, contributed to my expedition by my New Zealand friend in London, Guy Ashton, which proved extremely useful, for they dealt with a series of situations that would have added further problems to my day. They satisfied my hunger, were made of nutritious, energy-rich ingredients and were small, light and delicious, so it was easy to stuff a few into my camera bag or pocket and forget about cooking. Highly recommended for any explorer's kit.

As the Indians' initial reticence faded they began approaching me with little gifts of fruit and firewood, small fish and the brightly coloured feathers of the parrots and birds of paradise they plucked and ate as if they were chickens. We bathed together in the crystal stream, one of the main delights of the Amazon, and went upstream to collect its pure mineral water for drinking. I discarded my water filter and the nasty-tasting Micropure pills and never once got ill. I gave them biscuits and shared with them my early morning ginger tea, brewed on an open fire, and day by day, hour by hour, I quietly inserted myself into their lives. My cameras always at the ready, I picked out my images from the treasure trove that spread around me.

Lori Var gently but firmly let me know that he did not want me to photogaph his last baby. Each time I approached his hammock with my camera he covered the child with his arms and smilingly signalled to me to move on. I never found out the reason for his reticence, as he himself did not mind being photographed, so I deduced that it was probably to do with the ancient fear that photographs rob people of their souls or bring sickness by interfering with the spirits. It was only Lori Var and his family who acted thus: the other families of the *maloca* did not seem to mind. Perhaps it was because he was the shaman of the group. I shall never know.

To protect my Olympus cameras and lenses from humidity and dust I always put them carefully away in their foam-lined case, which remained tightly closed when I was not using them. One morning I noticed to my amazement that the viewfinder was filled with tiny red ants which completely obliterated the image in front of me. When I removed the lens the tiny insects were crawling all over the complex and delicate mechanism inside. How they got there remains a mystery to this day. Not only did they penetrate the case, but they also managed to enter the camera behind the lens and – even more baffling – once inside they squeezed in behind the little inner mirror that bounces the image to the viewfinder.

It was hard, relentless work, but I felt glad and satisfied at being able to cope in a world that was so alien to my own.

Dekka would come every few days to visit us. Through her I was able to gauge the degree to which I was accepted, and together we managed to some extent to breach the difficult language barrier which limited our dialogues to smiles and signs and a few words of Portuguese. The nights were always the most difficult to handle, for they started at approximately six o'clock when it got dark, and with only my torch and some candles there was not much I could do. I had brought along a lot of books, which did often save my sanity, but the effort of trying to read in a small tent by candle or torchlight soon defeated me, so I would just lie in the dark and listen to the sounds of night in the *maloca*. These were many and varied – croaking toads, barking dogs, crying children and hooting night owls, mingled with much loud coughing and spitting, and the occasional ripple of laughter which rang like a haunting crystal bell through the night. I have never heard such a bewitching sound: it resembled the call of some magical bird, filled with joy and melody.

Then there were the endless conversations lasting way into the night which were sometimes carried out across the compound, but which were never jarring or too loud. As in everything else, the Indians managed to keep a sense of harmony in the tones of their voices, and when they raised them it was always more of a call than a shout. The only exception was their communion with the healing spirits they summoned to cure the sick. This was the most singular and baffling affirmation of their roots, so close to the dawn of creation. With unwavering conviction, for hours at a time, they called on the spirits with loud, guttural animal grunts and shouts, inhaling and exhaling in unison with energetic gyrations and flailing of arms and legs. In the daytime this ritual was accompanied by the snorting of hallucinogenic snuff, which they blasted into each other's nostrils through bamboo pipes about two feet long. The ailing person would lie silent and motionless in the hammock, eyes closed, and completely abandoned to the mysterious spiritual forces, letting them wash over him or her in waves of sound and gestures. These loud incantations sometimes went on way into the night, and I would lie in bed praying for them to stop so I could get some sleep.

Small fires for cooking burned beside the hundred or so hammocks hung around the inner perimeter, kept alight by intermittent fanning with woven palm leaf fronds. This circle of flaming embers, glowing in the dark, turned the great arena into a dramatic backdrop for the Indians' powerful exhortations, and for me it all suddenly became believable.

I often sat with Dekka and Lori Var and talked about the significance of these happenings. His explanation translated into the sort of psycho-healing rituals familiar in our culture. There were of course certain maladies brought by the whites, he explained, which the spirits were not familiar with and could not heal, such as malaria and tuberculosis, and until the white man brought his medicines the victims of these diseases simply died. No wonder there were no longer any old people around, I thought. Lori Var explained how the spirits of the dead are passed on by the living when the ashes of their cremated bones are consumed by the surrounding community in a ritual ceremonial feast of banana porridge. The dead person is wrapped in his or her hammock and hung up high in a tree near to the *maloca*. The body is left there until it has decomposed and only the bones remain. These are then burned in the centre of the *maloca* and ground to ashes. A feast day is set, and runners with invitations to join the feast are sent out to the surrounding *malocas*, often as far as a week's walk away.

I witnessed these arrivals and departures while standing in the wings listening to Lori Var, who by now had become my friend, as he gave or received the news carried to and from the outer reaches of the surrounding forest. These were always emotional moments for me as I tried to imagine the route these messengers travelled, sometimes for several days, sleeping when night fell in hammocks slung between the trees – never on the ground because of deadly insects and snakes – hunting and fishing for sustenance and drinking from the streams. It was all done so matter of factly, and was simply part of their daily lives. How far would we, who have strayed from our origins, be capable of living like these people, I wondered, when I was having difficulty dealing even with the minor, superficial discomforts of the insects and heat? For me watching these people live put everything back into its right perspective, and reminded me yet again of the importance of preserving this way of life. This was perhaps why I was there to record its images.

One evening, swinging in my hammock listening to my new Yanomami's symphony, I felt a shadow approach from behind. I looked round and recognized Genesio, who came to me and in a soft, shy voice greeted me, and then asked me in his broken Portuguese if 'I would like to go and play with him.' Not quite understanding what he meant, I asked him to repeat his question, which he did without changing the tone of his voice, smiling like a child; a bit taken aback and not quite understanding if this perhaps was a gentle sexual advance, I declined as gently. 'All right ,' he said, and melted back into the shadows from which he had emerged. I asked Dekka about this next day and she told me that, no, it wasn't necessarily a sexual advance, he just wanted to play with me like he did with his friends, when they hopped and skipped around together whooping and calling to each other beneath the stars in the open centre of the *maloca*. Having never caught sight of the slightest sign of lovemaking I asked Dekka about it, and she explained to me that it is usually kept very private and carried out in the forest away from the other members of the *maloca*. Living as they do in their hammocks, I often wondered how the Indians carried out the act of love. I found out one night while I was staying with Nick Burch, when I got up to have a pee at three in the morning and saw a Surúi couple. The woman lay on her back in the hammock and the man straddled her with his feet on the ground on either side of the hammock. I returned to bed with a faint smile on my face. I had just learned something new.

The medical team from São Paulo who were working on Davi's project would come each day to treat the sick with a supply of white man's medicine covering a large spectrum of the more common ailments. With them I was able to delve a little further into the health problems afflicting the Yanomami. I made friends with Istran, the young Brazilian bush doctor heading the team, and had many fascinating chats with him as I watched him diagnose and treat the various forms of malaria, meningitis, flu and pneumonia that so often prove fatal to the Yanomami, who have little resistance to white maladies. Istran had worked a lot with them over the years and had a great deal of respect for their spiritual healings. In his view powers of suggestion and the psyche played an important role in their healing processes. His contact with the Yanomami had led him to investigate and study alternative medicine, and although he treated the Indians with conventional remedies, he understood and respected Lori Var's approach and was convinced that everything in medicine, as elsewhere in life, was interconnected. He was a man of total dedication, working in often harassing conditions. As I watched him manipulating a hand-held microscope splotlit by sunlight bouncing off a miniature mirror (a gift from Oxfam bought with funds collected in a school in Oxfordshire), or laying out blood slides at night, with a torch between his teeth, on a table made of stripped branches covered with a banana leaf, I felt much humbled by his pioneering spirit and energy.

It was interesting that, surrounded as I was by so many malaria cases, some of them of the lethal Falciparum kind, I never got infected by the mosquitoes that feasted on us or fell ill from the water I drank. After meeting Istran I stopped even taking prophylactics against malaria, as he explained to me that a body unaccustomed to medicine reacts much more favourably to medication when it is ailing. I had a long talk with Davi on this subject and he expounded at length on how the spirits help the white man's medicine. I found it difficult to relate to what Istran was telling me, but I knew he had been invited to lecture at the Medical University of São Paulo, where he kept a large audience hanging on his words.

I returned to São Paulo at the end of my three and a half month journey across Brazil exhausted and scarred by the jungle, having lost several kilos in weight and gained several years of knowledge and understanding, much enriched and exhilarated by the ordeal. I strolled through a small park near my hotel on my way to my rendezvous with Ailton Krenak. The sun poured through the leaves of the ancient trees still standing and now protected, the remnants of what had been a forest many years ago, before men came to build their sprawling, ugly city, replacing the trees with concrete.

On a bench fashioned from a glorious rich coloured trunk an old Indian proverb was etched, 'What we do to the earth, we do to the sons of the earth': thought-provoking words that seemed so simply to encapsulate the whole drama of the threatened world from which I had just emerged. I sat for a while on the bench and looked up at the leafy canopy above me, listening to the birds hidden among the branches. The traffic roared around me, but here in the park everything was very still. I closed by eyes, letting the primal, still unsullied images I had left behind tumble through my mind and wondered what it is in man that makes him the only animal that destroys its own environment.

My contact with the Indians in the forest had definitely affected me, but I did not yet know to what extent. I was still too involved in the more immediate mundane issues of getting back home. It was only once I began sifting through my pictures and my film in London that a strong and undeniable feeling of emotional rapport began creeping into me, as the images I had captured sprang back at me. I felt a sudden surge of warmth and love for the Indians which is difficult to define. Although I had not recognized it at the time, it was evident how, even subconsciously, contact with these gentle people in their rarefied environment can and does affect one. It was a sobering observation and left me once again facing the dilemmas that the march of time inevitably carries in its wake; the destruction of innocence.

Was this perhaps the reason why I travel so far to try and capture it before it has all gone; to freeze and preserve it for the next generation who will not be as fortunate as I to have witnessed it first hand?

I often caught myself wondering about the final objective of my enterprise as I watched the Indians' lives unfold around me. Recording this way of life with my camera would preserve it in some small way, if only in the pages of a book, but at the same time it would draw attention to it and expose it to the world outside. In what way would this affect them? However inevitable it might be, change would bring with it disturbances and problems that would interfere with their way of life, creating needs and desires as yet unknown to them. Was I ultimately doing them a disservice? Now already the first signs of irrevocable change had begun to creep in. How much longer before it will all have gone?

Overleaf A Yanomami hunter emerges from the forest dressed in ceremonial regalia. The Yanomami, who live on the remote southern slopes of the Guiana Highlands on the border between Brazil and Venezuela, are one of the last great Indian nations of Amazonia to remain relatively isolated from the outside world, but are now also threatened by western policies.

THE YANOMAMI

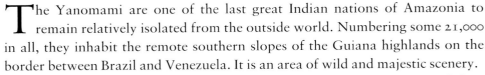

The Yanomami are one of the last great Indian nations of Amazonia to remain relatively isolated from the outside world. Numbering some 21,000 in all, they inhabit the remote southern slopes of the Guiana highlands on the border between Brazil and Venezuela. It is an area of wild and majestic scenery.

In places high sandstone mesas thrust clear of the rolling hills to reveal their weathered crowns. The hills themselves, which rise to over a 1000 metres on the watersheds, are clothed in a dense cover of lush, cool rainforest. In this steep country, dissected by small streams and plunging rivers, the Indians travel mainly on foot along a network of scarcely visible paths that link the widely scattered communities.

Since the middle of the last century the Yanomami have experienced a major demographic expansion, moving out from the hills on the watershed between the headwaters of the Orinoco and the Amazon's northern tributaries. They now live in about 360 villages spread out over a huge area of over 75,000 square miles (about 190,000 square kilometres) – an area the size of Nebraska. This expansion has brought them down near to the major rivers, where some Yanomami have adopted cassava as a staple and learned to make canoes.

The Yanomami have long been famous as a warrior people. They are notable for using remarkably long bows and arrows, and their reputation among the neighbouring tribes for bravery is matched only by the respect accorded their shamans. The Yanomami have evoked strong reactions from all who have lived with them.

Rapids and major waterfalls on all the rivers draining the Yanomami's homeland kept them in almost complete isolation from the outside world until the 1950s. The isolation was shattered with the arrival of light aircraft which allowed missionaries to set up stations throughout their territory, and since then the tempo of change has escalated inexorably.

In the 1960s Brazilian diamond prospectors began pushing through the Yanomami's eastern territories, bringing in venereal diseases, tuberculosis and racist exploitation. Repeated contacts with the outside world brought in shattering new epidemics. Outbreaks of measles swept away up to 20% of the Yanomami in some villages and the Yanomami's numbers started to decline.

In 1973, the assault on the Yanomami homeland intensified with the building of the BR-210 Perimetral Highway across the lowland forests in the south of their territory. Despite protests by concerned anthropologists and priests, Brazil's military government thrust the road through the Indians' lands without taking any measures to protect them from the consequences. Repeated epidemics reduced the population of some villages by up to 90%. The survivors adopted a pathetic existence of roadside nomadism, begging for food and goods from passing vehicles. Inevitably, venereal diseases spread to the demoralized Indians during these lay-by encounters.

The radar mapping of Amazonia also revealed the likelihood of rich mineral deposits in the Yanomami's heartland, exciting the avarice of would-be miners. In the mid-1970s a cassiterite find brought some 3000 miners into the very centre

The Yanomami remained almost completely isolated from the outside world until the 1950s. Similarities in face and body decoration, among other things, indicate however that there have for a long time been contacts between different Indian peoples. This Bororo man, photographed earlier this century, wears a string belt and feather decorations in his ears that are very similar to those worn by the Yanomami.

of the Yanomami area. More epidemics ensued, and conflicts, caused by miners taking Yanomami women and food, led to several deaths.

The government forced the miners to withdraw and, under pressure from concerned academics and the Catholic church, set about securing land for the Indians. However, the government's solution, to create twenty-one small and isolated reserves allowing non-Indian settlement and mining in the intervening areas, caused an international outcry.

While the Brazilian government vacillated, pressure from the miners escalated. Illegal prospectors moving through the Yanomami area found stream beds rich in alluvial gold. Numbers of illegal miners in the Yanomami area gradually increased, until by the late 1980s there were some 40,000 miners and camp-followers on the Indians' land. Deaths from epidemics soared, leading to the loss of about a sixth of the Brazilian Yanomami's total numbers. Mercury spills from the mines polluted the rivers and poisoned fish and drinking water. Conflict between Indians and miners led to numerous killings and revenge deaths. Miners took to shooting Indians indiscriminately, even to the point of blasting hiding Yanomami children out of the trees.

Intense international campaigns in support of Yanomami demands to remove the miners and secure their territory as a single continuous 'Indian Park' have eventually begun to have an effect. In 1989 a Yanomami leader, Davi Kobenawa, was presented the Global 500 award by the United Nations for his defence of his peoples' lands and their environment. Yet the mining invasion was then at its very height. In receiving his award, Davi said:

> I am not against gold prospectors. I am against gold prospecting, because it makes holes and ruins the river and the river channels. The Yanomami do not do that, cut the ground, cut the trees, burn the forest. We are not enemies of nature because we live out there in the jungle. It takes care of our health. Omao, our ancestral hero, gave us the land to live on, not to sell. Whites sell and go to another place. Indians do not do that. . . . Now the fish are suffering, the rivers are being destroyed. Even the Whites are suffering up there. Indian and White, poor White and rich White. Because the sickness is not afraid, it kills anybody – the rich, the brave, the big ones. My land is the last land to be invaded, it is the last invasion. After the Indian suffers, the White will suffer too. And then the war will come among you . . .

In early 1991, the Brazilian President made a renewed promise to secure the Yanomami's land as a single large area. If this promise is made effective the Yanomami may be set on a road to recovery. Those on the other side of the border, whose lands have not suffered an invasion on the same scale, have also begun to ask for title to their land and there are signs that the Venezuelan government may accede to their demand. The Indians are organizing into cooperatives producing honey and vegetables for the local markets. Although there is no place yet for optimism, there are glimmers of hope that the Yanomami are through the worst. Even so, international support for their struggle will be crucial for a long while yet.

Pages 160-3 Children of the forest. Growing up in the security of the *maloca*, where they play together in complete freedom and are affectionately indulged by the adults, Yanomami children display enormous confidence and spirit.

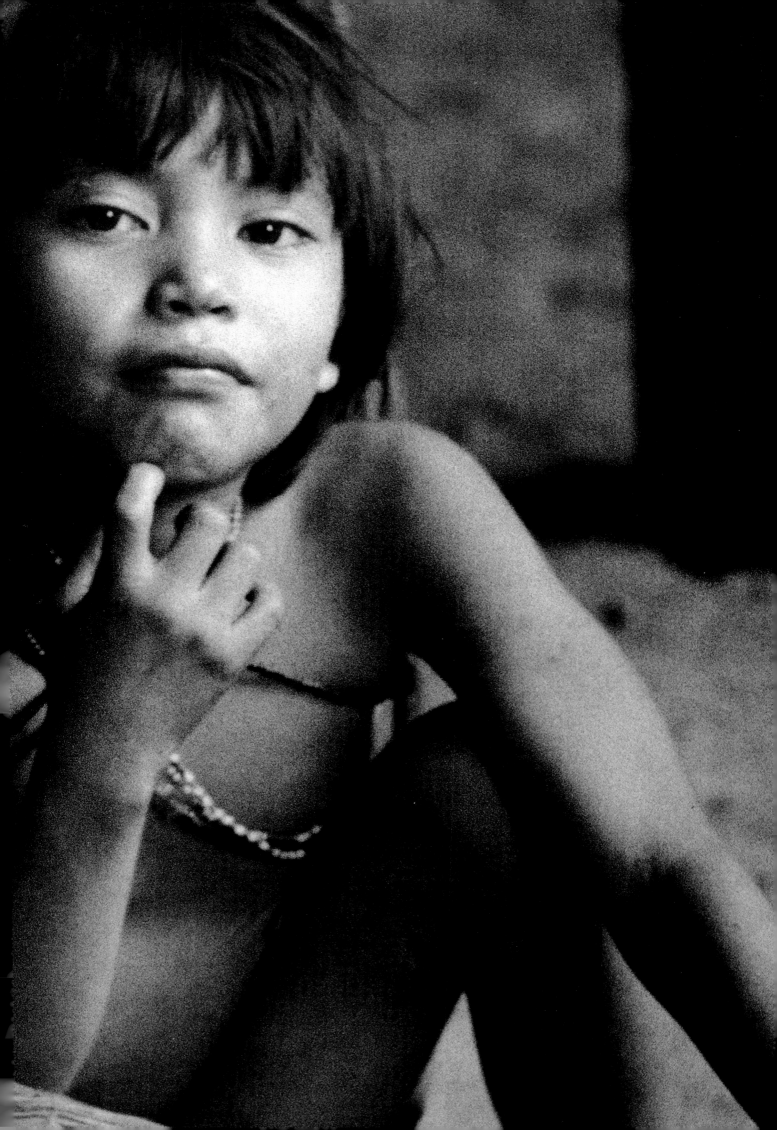

Preceding pages Cassava, bananas and sugar cane are among the
food crops cultivated in small plots cleared among the trees.
Yanomami methods of cultivation are singularly well suited to the
poor soils of the forest. Once cleared and planted their gardens are
hardly 'weeded', but gradually become overgrown and reabsorbed
into the forest as the crops are harvested. Meanwhile another
garden will have been cleared in a different part of the forest, so
that no area becomes exhausted and barren. The Indians have an
unerring memory for the sites of their former gardens, and will
return over several years to harvest crops such as peach palms
which take a while to come to maturity.

Above, opposite and pages 168-9 Yanomami children in the forest. From the age of five boys occasionally accompany their fathers on hunting expeditions, while girls help their mothers with cultivating and preparing and other domestic chores. Apart from this they are free to roam the forest and splash about in the river at will.

Pages 170-1 The little string aprons worn by the girls and women have a variety of uses.

Preceding pages String hammocks slung from poles inside the *maloca* are the Yanomami's only furniture. They are woven on large vertical frames by strapping four poles together.

Above and pages 176–9 Hammocks slung round a fire define each family's space, or hearth, within the *maloca*. The fires, which are kept burning night and day, punctuate the shady perimeter of the great circular building. The smoke curls upwards towards the roof made of overlapping leaves, where it hangs for a while, deterring winged insects, before drifting out of the large central opening. Beneath is a large open space, the arena for communal rituals, dancing and children's play. The all-purpose hammocks, meanwhile, are occupied by people nursing or playing with children, chatting, decorating each other, spinning or catching up with sleep.

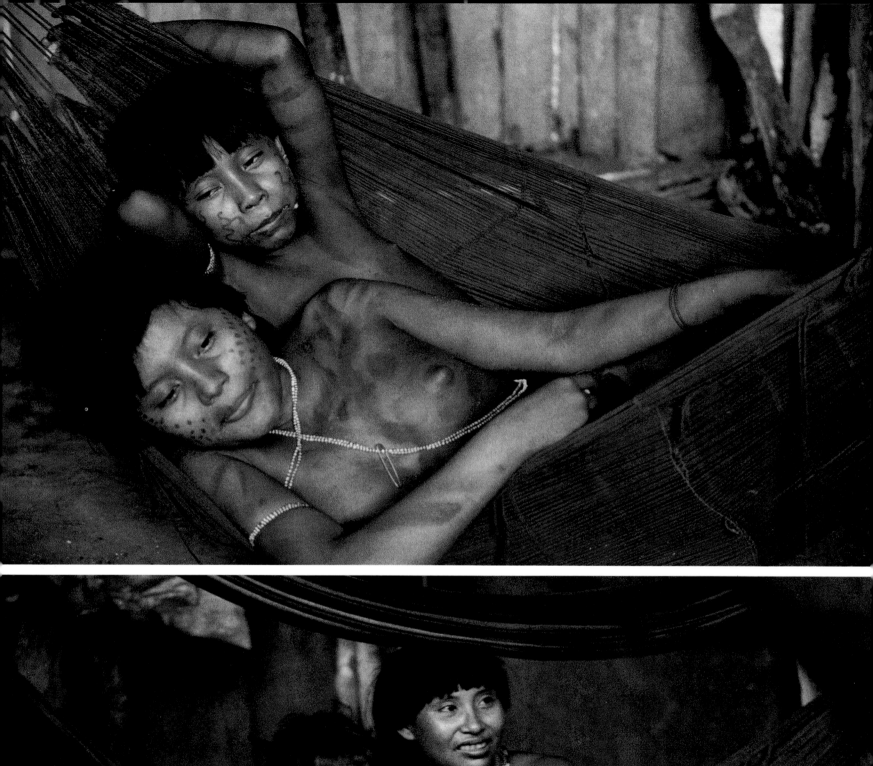

Above and opposite The *maloca* is the centre of Yanomami life, where nearly all social and work activities take place. Utensils made from materials gathered in the forest, like this basket being woven from lianas, are hung round each family hearth. Basketwork, weaving and the making of kitchen utensils are all women's work, while men are responsible for making hammocks and weapons and undertaking any woodwork or building work, such as repairs to the structure of the *maloca*. Women are also responsible for the complex preparations required to make cassava edible.

Preceding pages, above and opposite Hunting is strictly for
the men, either alone or in pairs. Lori Var would stand absolutely
motionless waiting for birds to settle in the trees. The Yanomami
are renowned for their immense skill in the use of their longbows
and poison-tipped arrows, but take care never to kill more than
they need to for fear that they will be haunted by the vengeful
spirits of the dead animals. Every time they kill an animal or take
produce from the forest they believe they incur a debt, which must
be repaid.

Preceding pages To the forest peoples virtually all the animals of the forest represent a valuable supplement to their diet, but of all prey the relatively rare larger forest mammals – tapir, peccaries, deer and giant anteater – are the most prized.

Left As they play in the forest, Indian children gradually become familiar with its astonishing variety of plant and animal life. By the time they are grown up they will not only have become skilled hunters, but will also be able to recognize hundreds of individual species of useful plants, indispensable as sources of food, medicines, drugs, dyes, poisons and materials for making buildings, ropes, hammocks, weapons, utensils and more. It has been estimated that tropical rainforests contain more than half of the world's species of flora and fauna.

Pages 190–1 and 194–5 From the clearing that surrounds the *maloca* narrow paths lead to the forest in all directions. The most clearly defined, leading to the river and the cultivated gardens, are used daily. More difficult to distinguish are those that are used less frequently, leading to other *malocas*, several hours' or perhaps days' march away. Yet others, leading into the depths of the forest, are visible only to the trained eye of a hunter, marked simply by a broken twig or a snicked liana there. Prey is carried home slung on the hunter's back.

Pages 192–3 In the normal cycle of the rainforest death is the source of new life: as plant and animal life decays a host of fungi and different micro-organisms sets to work to break it down and release its nutrients for other plants to take up. Every species in the forest is part of a self-contained and extraordinarily efficient recycling system. If the cycle is broken precious minerals and nutrients will leach away, and the weak soil will be unable to support life.

Right Trickling, dripping, pouring in
tropical storms, rushing in great rivers or
lying still in swamps and marshes, water is
the life-blood of the rainforest. For centuries
it was also the Yanomami's bastion against
incursions by outsiders, as the only access to
their territory was up rivers whose rapids
and waterfalls made them impossible to
navigate. Not until the arrival of light
aircraft in the 1950s was their isolation
shattered.

Overleaf Lori Var in the forest. The
kernels of the purple fruit tied to his back
contain a bright red paste which the Indians
use for body decoration. In the competitive
world of the rainforest, plants vie with each
other to produce dazzlingly eye-catching
fruit and seeds which will attract the
animals on which they depend to spread the
seeds. The Indians turn these brilliant
pigments to their own uses.

Pages 200–5 Macaws, toucans, guans,
tangers and other spectacular forest birds
are plucked, skinned and put in the cooking
pot like chickens. The feathers are carefully
set aside to be stitched into magnificent
headdresses and other decorations
(overleaf).

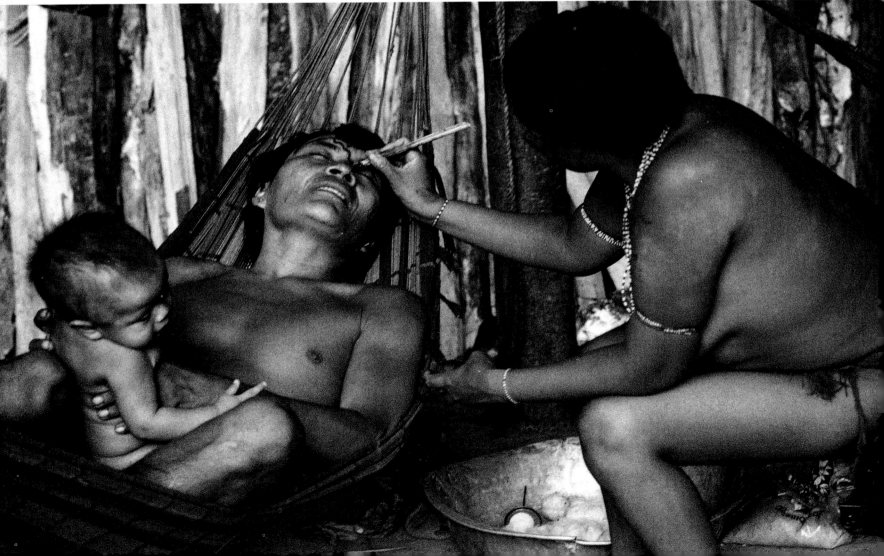

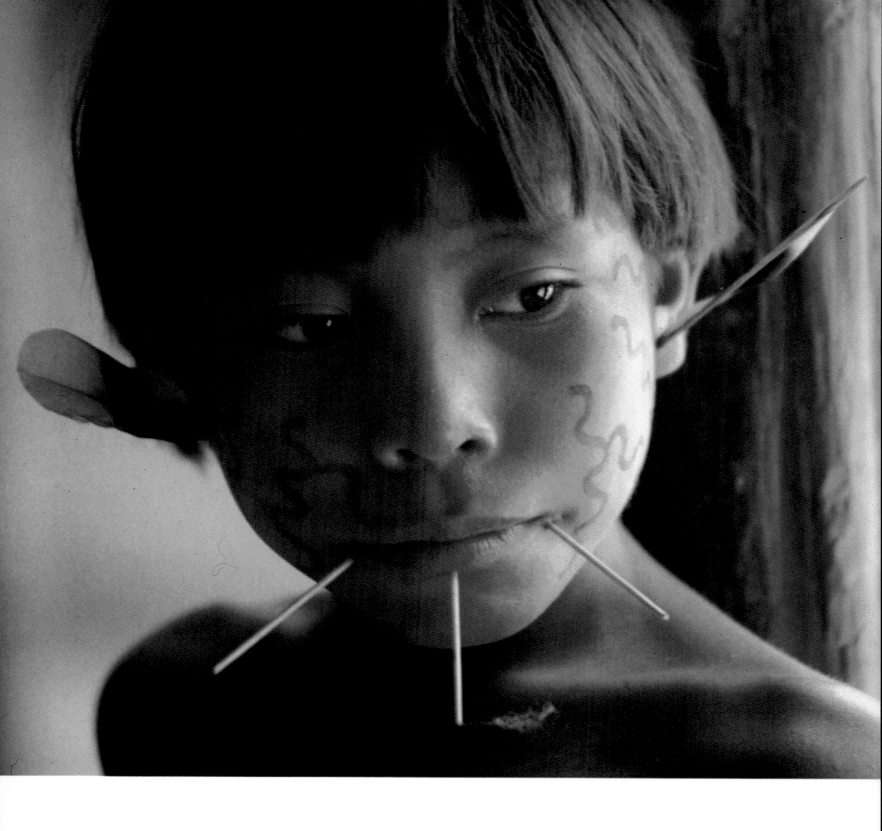

Pages 206-15 Painting each other is a social activity of great importance. Designs are based on geometrical and natural motifs, adapted according to the skill of the artist and the contours of the face or body to be painted. Sometimes a visit to a neighbouring *maloca* will provide ideas for new patterns which will suddenly become popular. Red dyes are the most usual, with black being reserved generally to indicate either mourning or bravery. Body decoration is used to convey coded messages, veiled or overt, between lovers and courting couples. Women adorn themselves not only with paint and feathers, but also with scented leaves and flowers; in addition women and children pierce their lower lips and noses with sharpened sticks.

215

Above, opposite and preceding pages Festivities in the
maloca. For this more or less impromptu dance of welcome the
preparations were relatively simple. On more formal or solemn
occasions everyone may spend days preparing food and drink.
Often these festivities are arranged between *malocas*: messengers
are despatched through the forest with invitations, and answers are
eagerly awaited before the excited preparations can begin. For the
Yanomami these occasions are an important opportunity to
demonstrate their generosity and hospitality towards other
malocas, and huge quantities of banana soup, plantain and smoked
meat, manioc beer and manioc bread are prepared to last
throughout the festivities, which may last as long as four or five
days.

So closely are the Indians' lives bound up with their environment that any interference with or damage to either the forest or the rivers threatens their very existence.

Opposite The cultivation and preparation of cassava, the staple food crop, is the most time-consuming of the women's chores. It is also among the most important, as without careful processing the cyanide compound-bearing tubers would be poisonous.

Above, opposite and overleaf Ingenious arrangements of baskets and slings allow women to carry heavy loads of plantain, bananas or cassava as well as their babies, while sometimes even managing to keep both hands free as well. Parents observe strict dietary restrictions and avoid sex in order to protect their children' spirits, and the illness or death of a newborn child is felt as a calamity by the whole community. Children have several spirits, the chief of which comes from the father's sperm and lives in the child's chest, heart and blood. In addition every child has a second spirit, which takes the form of an animal: harpy eagles for boys and weasels for girls. For this reason the hunting of either of these animals is forbidden.

Above, opposite and overleaf While the men go hunting the women – accompanied as always by their babies – gather cultivated crops from their gardens and wild plants from the forest. Women also gather smaller but nutritious animal life, from frogs and land crabs to termite larvae and caterpillars.

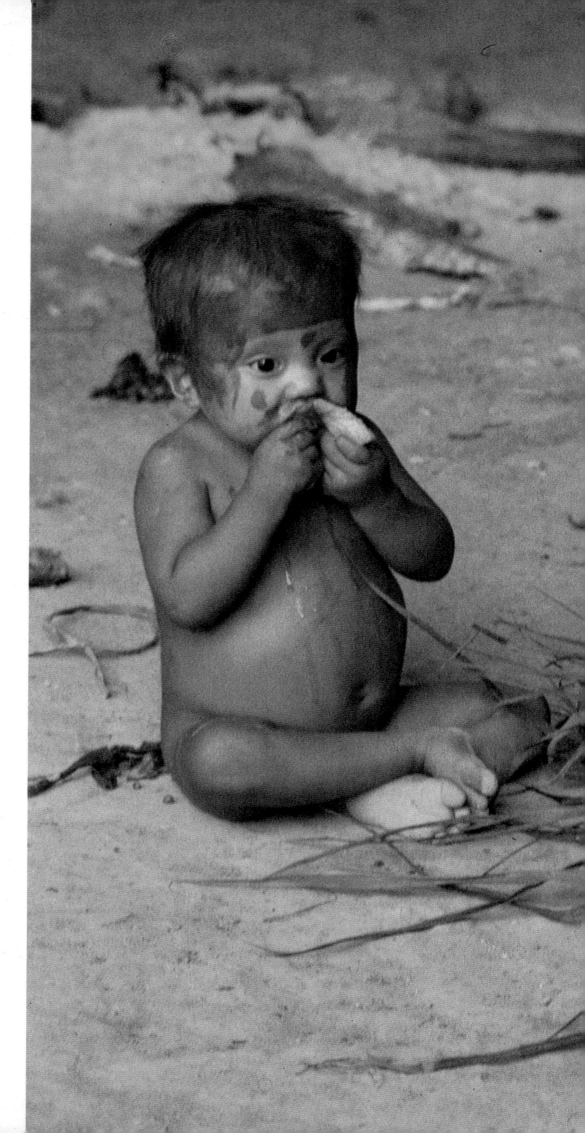

Pages 230-3 The camaraderie born of communal living is constantly evident among the children, who transform the *maloca* into a huge playground during the daytime. Bands of children tear to and fro across the central space with apparently inexhaustible energy, swinging from the hammocks, shinning up the poles that support the roof, playing at hunting and setting up miniature 'hearths', where with tremendous concentration they manage to light little fires over which they cook their hapless prey. Meanwhile quiet little groups will be getting on with the important and absorbing daily task of grooming each other.

Right and preceding pages The fruits of the forest, eaten either raw or boiled in water, are an important part of the Indians' diet. As many of the fruit grow at the very top of palm trees as much 60 feet or so (20 metres) tall, games involving scaling the poles of the *maloca* are perfect practice. Often the children will chase each other up and down fearlessly, pretending to be jaguars or other fierce animals, and sometimes binding their feet together with lianas in order to get a better purchase.

We have lived in this place for a long time, a very long time, since the
time when the world did not yet have this shape. We learned with the ancients
that we are a tiny part of this immense universe, fellow travellers with all the
animals, the plants and the waters. We are all a part of the whole;
we cannot neglect or destroy our home.

Ailton Krenak

BIBLIOGRAPHY

Branford, Sue and Glock, Oriel *The Last Frontier: fighting over land in the Amazon*, Zed Books, London, 1985

Carmichael, Elizabeth, Hugh-Jones, Stephen, Moser, Brian and Tayler, Donald, *The Hidden Péoples of the Amazon*, British Museum Publications, London, 1985

CEDI, *Povos Indigenas no Brasil: Javari*, Centro Ecumenico de Documentacao e Informacao, São Paulo, 1981

Cohen, J.M., *The Four Voyages of Christopher Columbus*, Penguin, Harmondsworth, 1969

Colchester, Marcus, 'Myths and Legends of the Sanema', *Antropologica* 56:25–127, 1981

—, 'The cosmovision of the Venezuelan Sanema', *Antropoligica* 58:97–174, 1982

Gray, Andrew, *The Amerindians of South America*, Minority Rights Group, London, 1989

Hanbury-Tenison, Robin, *Aborigines of the Amazon Rain Forest*, Time-Life Books, 1982

Hemming, John, *Red Gold*, Macmillan, London, 1978

Lizot, Jacques, *Tales of the Yanomami*, Cambridge University Press, 1985

Narby, Jeremy, 'Visions of Land: the Ashaninca and Resource Development in the Pichis Valley in the Peruvian Central Jungle', Ph.D. Dissertation, Stanford University, 1989

—, *The Rainforests: A Celebration*, Barrie & Jenkins, London, 1989

—, *A Tribute to the Forest People of Brazil*, The Gaia Foundation, London, 1990

Wilbert, Joahnnes and Simoneau, Karin (eds), *Folk Literature of the Yanomami Indians*, Latin America Center Publications, University of California, Los Angeles, 1990

INDEX